clothing, upholstery

GW00417788

Contents

Introduction	3
Chemicals	5
General Household	15
Bathroom	31
The Kitchen & Food	37
Laundry & Bleach	55
Outside, DIY & Pets	77
Hints, Tips & Stain Types	83
Index	89

All rights reserved,

No part of this publication may be reproduced, stored in a retrieval system or transmitted by any means (electronic, mechanical, photocopying or otherwise) without the prior permission of the publisher.

Text by Sara Burford

This edition published in 2009 by L&K Designs.

© L&K Designs 2009

PRINTED IN CHINA

Publishers Disclaimer

The uses, hints, tips and ideas contained in this book are passed on in good faith and the publisher cannot be held responsible for any adverse effects.

Introduction

Wouldn't you just love a world where we didn't have to deal with stains? One where spills, slips and messy accidents either didn't occur, or just didn't matter? One where we could just shrug when our 2-year old drops their chocolate ice-cream on the cream living room carpet, or where we could just turn over for another 5 minutes snooze in bed, even though we've just dropped coffee all over the duvet… sounds blissful.

Unfortunately, this stain-free Utopia is never going to happen! Stains are an unavoidable part of life – in fact, Benjamin Franklin's saying about life's only certainties being, 'death and taxes' should be extended to include stains! Anyone with children or pets will probably experience them on a regular, if not daily, basis.

But even for those without pets and children, we all know that awful moment of watching something drop, in what feels like painfully slow motion, all over something that we just know is going to be a nightmare to clean! Followed swiftly, by the sheer panic of not knowing how to treat the stain and worrying that we might make it worse through our good, but ignorant, intentions. It's certainly hard not to react in panic and scrub the stain with all our might, when that's actually the last thing we should be doing, (think red wine or coffee!).

So, we know we've got to put up with them, but how do we deal with them quickly, but effectively? Well, this is a great place to start! Having a good knowledge of these stain removal methods is a valuable tool to have under anyone's belt; and one which will importantly teach you what not to do, as much as what you need to do.

 This symbol indicates 'Eco Friendly' solutions

Stain Removal Must-Haves!

Before you start any stain-removing-action here are some must-haves for a successful stain-onslaught!

- Baby wipes
- Blotting paper
- Clean, dry cloths
- Small clothes brush
- Cotton wool
- Droppers (e.g. eye droppers)
- Eucalyptus Oil
- Goggles
- Kitchen paper towel
- Mild non-alkaline detergent
- Mouth & nose mask
- Proprietary Grease
- Protective gloves
- Scraper
- Trigger spray bottle, or mister
- Strong detergent
- Tea Tree Oil
- Spoon, spatula or blunt knife

 Where you see this symbol, you will find 'eco friendly' solutions.

Chemicals

Stain Removing Chemicals

Acetone

Classically the main component in nail polish remover, acetone is a widely used solvent; dissolving products such as nail polish, lacquers, adhesives and superglue. It is not suitable for use on fabrics such as acetate or tri-acetate rayons, or crease-resistant cottons.

An effective degreaser, it can also safely remove residues from glass and porcelain – as well as working wonders on permanent marker ink stains.

Useful for: *Removing nail polish and nail glue stains.*

Where to buy it: *DIY stores, Pharmacies.*

Ammonia (Household)

"Household" ammonia, or ammonium hydroxide, is a solution of ammonia mixed in water, (ranging from 5 to 10% ammonia). Ammonia can be used as a household cleaning aid and in stain removal remedies.

Ammonia has an instantly recognisable, pungent smell and caution should be exercised when using it. Contact will cause irritation to the mucous membranes, eyes and skin. It should never be mixed with any product containing bleach, as this can create hazardous gases – which are potentially fatal.

Care should be taken when using with fabrics, as fabrics and colours may be damaged if not properly diluted.

Useful for: *Removing a wide variety of stains, including;*
          mould, chocolate, fruit juices, oil, grease and blood.

Where to buy it: *Pharmacies, DIY stores, supermarkets.*

Chlorine Bleach

When laundering tough stains, using a stronger bleaching agent, such as chlorine bleach, may sometimes be necessary. The process of bleaching removes and fades colour, so is highly effective at removing stains.

Chlorine Bleach cont/

However, care should be taken with coloured and delicate fabrics, as damage and discolouration may occur. Never mix chlorine bleach with other products or natural cleaning remedies.

Useful for: *Removing stains such as; fruit, berries, deodorants & antiperspirants, food colouring, grass and mildew.*

Where to buy it: *Supermarkets, DIY stores. Chlorinated laundry bleach can be purchased in supermarkets.*

Dry-Cleaning Fluid

Also known as tetrachloroethylene, this colourless liquid is primarily used as a solvent in the dry cleaning process. It is often used in spot removing solutions and paint strippers and can be utilised as an effective stain remover. It is nonflammable, but should only be used in well ventilated areas as inhalation may cause unwanted side effects, such as headache, dizziness and nausea. Read the manufacturers instructions carefully before use.

Useful for: *Removing difficult to shift stains, such as; butter, ice-cream, chewing gum, crayon, shoe polish and candle wax.*

Where to buy it: *DIY stores, online.*

Glycerine

The low-toxicity chemical compound glycerol is more commonly known as glycerine and is consumed for use as a clear, odourless liquid. Used as a cleaning aid, glycerine is useful in softening older and more stubborn stains. It will not damage or diminish fabrics and colours when applied.

Useful for: *Removing stains such as; grease, alcohol, coffee & tea, perfume, scorch marks and tobacco.*

Where to buy it: *Pharmacies, supermarkets.*

Hydrogen Peroxide

Used primarily as a bleaching agent, hydrogen peroxide is a popular household cleaning aid. Much milder than chlorine bleach, this colourless

Hydrogen Peroxide cont/

liquid can be used as a disinfectant and is useful in removing stubborn stains, although care should be taken with delicate fabrics and colours.

Useful for: *Removing stubborn stains, such as; blood, urine, tea & coffee and grass.*

Where to buy it: *Pharmacies.*

Methylated Spirits (Denatured Alcohol)

Also known as wood alcohol, this inexpensive and useful liquid solvent is useful for removing grass, resin and ink stains, (from non-porous surfaces and fabrics). For use on acetate fabrics and non-colourfast materials, the solution should be diluted to third strength. Care should be taken on wooden surfaces, as this solution may damage 'finished' surfaces. Methylated spirits are poisonous – so take care when storing.

Useful for: *Removing stains such as; red wine, greasy marks, tar, ink, paint, PVA glue and candle wax.*

Where to buy it: *DIY stores, Pharmacies.*

Rubbing Alcohol

Referring to either the chemical compound of isopropyl alcohol or ethyl alcohol, rubbing alcohol can be used as a stain removal solution. Rubbing alcohol is poisonous; therefore care should be taken as poisoning can occur from ingestion, inhalation and contact. Always wear protective gloves and do not mix with other cleaning products.

Useful for: *Removing stains such as; grease spots, paint, permanent marker and lipstick.*

Where to buy it: *Pharmacies, DIY stores.*

Turpentine

A distilled resin originating from trees, (mainly pine trees), turpentine can be used to remove stains created by tar, wood resins and paint.

Useful for: *Removing stains from enamel and porcelain surfaces, such as baths, sinks and toilets. Also removes rust from metal.*

Turpentine cont/

Where to buy it: *DIY stores, online.*

White Spirit
A derivative of paraffin; this clear, transparent liquid is a commonly used solvent in painting and decorating – used primarily for cleaning paint brushes. It is also an effective cleaning and degreasing solvent, particularly useful in certain stain removal methods.

Useful for: *Removing stains such as; cooking oil, fruit jam, soap residue and paint.*

Where to buy it: *DIY stores, supermarkets.*

Eco-Friendly Chemicals

There are, without a doubt, some great stain removal products and chemicals that are readily available in most hardware and DIY stores, as well as in our supermarkets.

Unfortunately, as convenient as these wonder-products are, they also carry financial, environmental and most importantly, health costs. So if you're keen to keep it 'eco-friendly', here are a few natural wonder-products that will look after you and the environment – and keep those household costs down too!

Baking Soda
The chemical compound of baking soda is sodium bicarbonate; a white, solid natural mineral, most commonly consumed as fine, white powder. Also referred to as bicarbonate of soda, cooking soda and bread soda; this versatile powder is a staple in most kitchens.

As a cleaning aid, this non-toxic, mild abrasive cleaner is effective for scrubbing out stains, removing tarnish, softening hard water, neutralising acid and getting rid of nasty smells. Mixed with lemon juice, white vinegar or water – it makes a fantastic all-purpose cleaner and stain removing agent. It also works to deodorise unwanted smells created by stains.

Baking Soda cont/

Useful for: *Providing an effective scouring agent for removing stains such as; rust, tea & coffee, mildew, soap scum and pet urine.*

Where to buy it: *Supermarkets, food convenience stores.*

Beeswax

Beeswax is secreted by worker bees whilst building the honeycomb and can be used as a natural, sweet-scented cleaning product. Traditionally used in wood polishes, it can also be used to remove rust from iron.

Useful for: *For buffing wooden surfaces and removing rust stains.*

Where to buy it: *Supermarkets, online, specialised outlets.*

Borax

Also known as sodium borate, borax is a natural mineral and salt of boric acid. The clear crystals are odourless and can be mixed with most other cleaning agents, (check before use). A natural disinfectant and slightly more abrasive than baking soda; when mixed with lemon juice, water or white vinegar; borax is an excellent stain removing agent. Rinse surfaces and clothing thoroughly after use and do not use borax around food. Store well away from children and pets.

Safe for use with most fabrics, except wool.

Useful for: *Providing an effective scouring and stain removal agent for stains such as; limescale, rust, mildew, red wine, chocolate and coffee.*

Where to buy it: *Pharmacies, online.*

Cornflour

Cornflour is a useful 'absorbent' substance, (along with cornstarch and baking soda), for treating lighter, or new stains. Absorbents are particularly useful for new grease stains, as they soak up the excess grease and easily brush off. The light working of these substances won't damage the surfaces or fabrics they are applied to.

Cornflour cont/

Useful for:	*Removing new grease stains, crayon and mildew from books.*
Where to buy it:	*Supermarkets, food convenience stores.*

Cream of Tartar

A natural derivative of the winemaking process, potassium bitartrate is more commonly known as cream of tartar. Used for cleaning and stain removal, it can be mixed with liquids such as white vinegar, to make an effective cleaning paste.

Useful for:	*Removing stains such as; copper, rust, egg, fruit, red berries and grass.*
Where to buy it:	*Supermarkets, food convenience stores.*

Lemon Juice

When we think of lemons we're likely to think of words such as; fresh, sharp, zesty, zingy, crisp, refreshing… all words that we associate with a clean environment. But not only do they smell great, their mild acidic properties make them an inexpensive and natural bleaching agent, which makes them perfect for stain removal remedies. They also benefit us with their valuable antibacterial and antiseptic properties.

Useful for:	*Removing stains such as; limescale, mildew, rust, curry, berries, dried on fruit and water marks.*
Where to buy it:	*Supermarkets, grocers, food convenience stores, farm shops.*

Saliva

It's an absolute no, to cleaning your children's face with saliva, (we've all been there), – but a definite yes, for fresh stains in the absence of any other method of stain removal! Your saliva contains valuable enzymes which can work to dissolve some stains – so start by spitting on the mark, (not great on a first date, but hey…), and then use your finger to gently loosen the stain. Rinse with a little cold water and blot dry. Treat, as per the appropriate remedy, once you are able.

Useful for:	*Treating most stains, as an initial step. Do not use on grease or oil stains.*

Salt

Salt is an excellent cleaning aid – either on its own or mixed with other substances. Found in just about every household, it's cheap, effective and great at cleaning and removing unwanted smells. Its stain removal potential makes it another must-have for your cleaning routines.

Useful for:	*Removing stains such as; baked on food and spills, egg, limescale, blood, mildew, grease and ink.*
Where to buy it:	*Supermarkets, food convenience stores.*

Sunlight

The most natural source of them all – the sun is a great, gentle alternative to using manufactured bleaching products. Wet the area, either with just water or a little lemon juice, (depending on the fabric type), and simply dry in the sun. Fabulous!

Useful for:	*Removing stains such as; grass, iodine, mildew and rust.*

White Vinegar

This acidic liquid is a powerhouse when it comes to household use! The active ingredient, acetic acid, has natural cleaning, descaling and deodorising properties, which make it perfect for stain removal remedies, such as limescale, mildew, collar grime and pet urine. An eco-friendly must-have for your stain removal arsenal!

Useful for:	*Removing stains such as; hard water spots, limescale, mould, mildew, soap scum, rust and cigarette burns.*
Where to buy it:	*Supermarkets, food convenience stores.*

Safety Precautions

Although the vast majority of stain removal products and chemicals are popularly used around the home, it is vital to be aware of the relevant health and safety issues relating to their contents and their safe and appropriate use. Chemicals may be flammable or toxic; or both. Here are a few safety tips to consider before use:-

Accidents
In the event of accident, always refer to the manufacturer labels for instruction – and/or consult medical advice immediately.

Application
Apply chemicals sparingly, with the least strength to complete the task.

Bleach & Ammonia
Bleach and ammonia should NEVER be mixed – this mixture produces lethal gasses.

Care Labels
Read ALL of the manufacturers label directions and warnings.

Cleaning Cloths
Cloths should be lint free.

Combination of Chemicals
Do not combine stain removal chemicals or products together; unless specifically directed to do so. This can result in producing hazardous toxic gasses.

Container Safety
Always store chemicals and products in their original containers and always ensure lids are secure after use.

Cool Units
Prior to cleaning ovens or hobs, be sure that the units are off and completely cooled.

Disposal

Always follow the manufacturer's instruction regarding disposal of containers and out of date products and chemicals. If in doubt, contact your local waste disposal site for advice.

Excess Products & Chemicals

Do not store excess amounts of chemicals and products. This poses a greater fire risk, as well as becoming a disposal and environmental issue.

Flammable Chemicals

Use highly flammable chemicals outdoors where possible.

Inhalation

Avoid inhaling toxic fumes by keeping a door or window open. Toxic fumes can cause illness; and may be potentially fatal.

Overspray

Be careful of overspray of chemicals and products on hard surfaces, it can make the floor slippery and dangerous.

Protective Wear

Wear protective gloves when handling chemicals and products.

Remedies

Do not store 'made-up' remedies, use or discard once mixed – unless the instructions recommend future use.

Rinsing

Always rinse chemicals and products off thoroughly where indicated – and before use of other chemicals and products.

Smoking, Heat & Flames

Do not smoke under any circumstances. Keep well away from naked flames, sparks, pilot lights, fires and other electrical outlets.

Solvent Storage
Do not use plastic containers to store solvents.

Solvent & Strong Alkali Protection
ALWAYS wear protective gloves when using solvents and strong alkalis. Keep hands well away from skin and eyes when using stain removal products and chemicals – flush immediately with water should any accidents occur. Always seek medical advice.

Storage Conditions
Store chemicals and products in a cool, dark place – or according to their manufacturer instructions. Do not use containers that have rusted.

Storage Safety
Keep products well away from children and pets. Do not store products and chemicals near food. NEVER store chemicals or products in drink bottles.

Usage
Use all products and chemicals for the purposes described by the manufacturers only.

General Household

General Household

Alcohol Spots – *on wooden furniture*
Rub with a cream metal polish, rubbing in the same direction as the wood grain. Finish by rubbing the area with a light wax polish.

Beer – *on carpets & upholstery*
Take a damp sponge and dab the stain with soda water. ❧

Or, sponge with a mixture of 1 teaspoon of mild detergent and 225ml, (1 cup), of luke warm water, followed by a mixture of 1/3 cup of white wine vinegar in 2/3 cup of water. Finish the process by sponging with cold, clean water. ❧

Blinds – *fabric*
You can remove some stains from fabric blinds by rubbing the area with a piece of bread. ❧

Blood – *on carpets & upholstery*
Apply a mixture of cold water and flour to fresh blood stains. Gently rub the stain and blot dry. Once the stain has dried completely any residue should just brush away. ❧

Or, sprinkle a layer of pepsin powder over the stain, leave and then brush off.

Or, for older stains, apply a little hydrogen peroxide to the area, rub and rinse with cold water. Blot dry.

Blood – *on mattresses*
A troublesome stain, to say the very least. Best treated whilst fresh and still wet, blood stains can become permanent, especially if allowed to dry. Dab the stain with hydrogen peroxide in a towel, (bearing in mind it will bleach the towel and the mattress). Work from the outside of the stain inwards, this will reduce the risk of the stain spreading. Do not use water as this will rupture the blood cells and spread the stain. The hydrogen peroxide will

Blood – *on mattresses* **cont/**
start to bubble, bringing up the stain, blot with a dry cloth. Repeat this process until the stain has been removed. It is advisable to test an inconspicuous area of the mattress before applying the treatment.

Books
Treat mildew-stained pages in books by dusting them with talcum powder or cornflour. Close the book for 3-4 days and then brush off the pages. ✄

Butter – *on carpets & upholstery*
Dab with a little dry-cleaning solvent and then sponge with a solution of 1 teaspoon of mild detergent and 225ml, (1 cup), of luke warm water.

Candle Wax – *on wood*
Soften the wax with a hairdryer and wipe off with a paper towel. Wipe the wood over with a solution of white vinegar and water. ✄

Candle Wax – *on carpets & upholstery*
Remove as much wax as you can and then place a piece of brown paper over the remaining stain; iron over the top with a warm iron. The wax will melt and the brown paper will soak up the residue. Keep moving the paper on each iron stroke and introduce a new piece of paper, if required. Repeat until the stain has lifted. ✄

Candle Wax – *on silver*
Remove candle wax from your silver candlesticks by warming the wax with a hairdryer and then peeling the wax off. ✄

Carpets - *Stain Removal 'Musts'*

Never rub stains – blot them only. Soak liquid spills up with dry, absorbent materials such as cloths, paper kitchen towel or tissues.

Solids should have the excess scraped up with a blunt knife, spoon or spatula, before treating the stain.

Work all stains from the outside, inwards – to avoid the stain spreading.

Rinse out stain removal remedies, but do not wet the area excessively, as this will develop into a water stain.

Always brush the pile after treating the stain.

Use a hair dryer to dry the stain spot. Take care not to burn the carpet.

Carpets & Upholstery
Firstly, for spills of any kind, remove as much of the substance as you can by either blotting it with paper kitchen towel, or by scraping it away with a blunt knife or spoon. Do not rub - this will ingrain the stain into the pile/fabric and it will damage the texture of carpets.

Ceramic
Get rid of coffee and tea stains, even burn marks, by rubbing the area with a damp, clean cloth dipped in bicarbonate of soda. ✿

Chalk – *on wallpaper*
Damp a cloth with liquid detergent and luke warm water and gently rub the stain.

Or, gently rub the area with a rubber eraser. ✿

Chewing Gum
Infuriating – but easy to deal with! Place some ice cubes inside a plastic sandwich bag, (or other plastic bag), and press down on the gum for 3-4

Chewing Gum cont/

minutes. The gum should freeze and come off easily. Dab the area with lemon juice and then wipe off any residue.

Or, rub the gum with smooth peanut butter and it'll miraculously shift! ✤

Or, dab with a little dry-cleaning solvent and then sponge with a solution of 1 teaspoon of mild detergent and 225ml, (1 cup), of luke warm water.

Or, for clothes, using a toothbrush or nailbrush, brush the gum with egg white and leave for 30 minutes. Wash as normal. ✤

Chocolate – *on carpets*

Sponge with solution of 1 teaspoon of mild detergent and 225ml, (1 cup), of luke warm water, followed by a solution of 1 tablespoon of ammonia mixed in 110ml, ($\frac{1}{2}$ cup), of water.

Sponge again with the first solution and finish by sponging with cold, clean water and pat dry.

Cigarette Burns – *on wood*

Sprinkle baking soda on the burn and moisten with a little white vinegar. Use a pencil eraser to gently rub over the mark. There will still be a mark, but the mark will be clean and treatable with some wood stain. ✤

Coffee & Tea – *on carpets or upholstery*

Treat fresh stains using a cloth and cold water; blot thoroughly with paper kitchen towel and leave to dry. ✤

For older stains, using a cloth, apply a mixture of liquid detergent mixed with hot water. Rinse with cold water and blot. Leave to dry.

Coffee Tables

Remove rings left by glasses, cups and mugs by applying petroleum jelly to the area and leaving it for 24 hours. Wipe off with a dry cloth. ✤

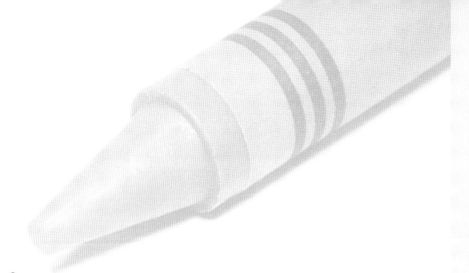

Crayon – *on carpets*
Sponge the area with a little dry-cleaning solvent, followed by a solution of one teaspoon of mild detergent and 225ml, (1 cup), of luke warm water. Finish by sponging with cold, clean water. 🌿

Crayon – *on painted walls*
Spray the affected area with lubricating oil and gently wipe off with paper. Sponge with bicarbonate of soda and gently rub the area in a circular motion. Wipe off with a clean, damp sponge and finish with a dry cloth. 🌿

Crayon – *on wallpaper*
Carefully scrape off any residual crayon and then cover with either blotting, or brown, paper. Iron the area on a warm setting, moving the paper round each ironing stroke, so that the stain can soak more effectively into the paper. Cover any residual stains with a paste of cornflour and water; leave to dry and then brush off. 🌿

Curry – *on carpets*
Shift curry stains by applying a mixture of lemon juice and water. 🌿

Dirt – *on carpets*
Sponge with solution of 1 teaspoon of mild detergent and 225ml, (1 cup), of luke warm water, followed by a solution of 1 tablespoon of ammonia mixed in 110ml, (½ cup), of water. Sponge again with the first solution and finish by sponging with cold, clean water. Pat dry.

Duvet cover

Prevent spills from staining your duvet. Mop the duvet cover immediately, to limit the amount of seepage through to the duvet underneath. Tie the stained section of the duvet cover off with an elastic band, (to keep it away from the duvet inside), and either sponge with cold water and washing detergent, or remove the cover completely and put through an appropriate wash cycle. ✿

Felt-Tip Pen

If you can't remove felt-tip pen marks with a damp cloth, then try dabbing a little methylated spirit onto a cloth and wiping the mark. Rinse off well with cold water.

Floor Tiles

This is a classic old remedy for removing built-up stains from water-based polishes and floor treatments. Make up a bucket of detergent solution, diluted in warm water and mop the area thoroughly. Follow this by moving around the area with a scrubbing brush, to remove the tidemark at the edge of the floor. Stubborn stains can be removed with a wire brush.

Fruit & Fruit Juice – *on carpets*

Sponge with solution of 1 teaspoon of mild detergent and 225ml, (1 cup), of luke warm water, followed by a solution of 1 tablespoon of ammonia mixed in 110ml, ($\frac{1}{2}$ cup), of water. Sponge again with the first solution and finish by sponging with cold, clean water and pat dry.

Glass Decanters

Fill the decanter with warm, soapy water and add 1 heaped tablespoon of salt and 1 cup of white vinegar. Leave for 3-4 hours, shaking the decanter occasionally. Rinse out and turn upside down on a clean, dry cloth to dry. ✿

Grease – *on carpet*
Sprinkle the grease spot with a good covering of corn starch and leave for 8-10 hours, (overnight would be fine). Vacuum the area, as normal.

Or, mix up 1 part salt to 4 parts rubbing alcohol and rub it on the grease stain, being careful to rub in the direction of the carpet's natural nap. ❧

Grease – *on wallpaper*
Mix some water and corn starch together in a bowl, into a paste-like consistency. Rub the area gently in a circular motion, with a soft cloth. Wipe over with a dry cloth. NB. It is advisable to test a small, inconspicuous area of the wallpaper before application. ❧

Grease – *on pathways, driveways & garage floors*
Remove grease stains from floors by sprinkling the area with bicarbonate of soda. Scrub well with a little warm water and a scrubbing brush and then rinse well. ❧

Greasy Fingers – *on wooden furniture*
Any household with children will be able to relate to this household occurrence! Ring a damp cloth in a solution of mild soap flakes and wipe the affected area. Buff dry with a dry, soft cloth.

Hard Water Spots – *on stainless steel*
Remove stubborn hard water spots by soaking a cloth in neat, white vinegar and rubbing the affected area. Rinse with cold water. ❧

Heat Marks – *on light coloured wooden furniture*
Mix together 1 part white toothpaste, with 1 part bicarbonate of soda and gently rub the mark, in a circular motion, with a soft, damp cloth. Wipe clean and buff with a little furniture polish. ❧

Or, make a paste from mayonnaise and ash and paint onto the affected area. Leave for 2-3 hours before removing. Buff the area with a damp cloth and then buff dry. ❧

Heat Marks – *on light coloured wooden furniture* **cont/**
Or, apply mayonnaise to the stain and leave for 8-10 hours. Wipe off with a dry cloth and buff gently. ✹

Heat Marks – *on polished furniture*
To remove heat marks on polished furniture, make up a paste from olive oil and ash. Apply to the marks and then rub off. ✹

Or, pour a little linseed oil on the marks and sprinkle with some sugar. Leave the sugar to absorb and then wipe off. ✹

Home Entertainment Systems
Remove greasy marks and stains by dampening a cloth with methylated spirits and gently rubbing the affected areas. Buff dry.

Ice-Cream – *on carpets*
Sponge with solution of 1 teaspoon of mild detergent and 225ml, (1 cup), of luke warm water, followed by a solution of 1 tablespoon of ammonia mixed in 110ml, ($\frac{1}{2}$ cup), of water. Sponge again with the first solution and finish by sponging with cold, clean water and pat dry.

Ink – *on carpets & upholstery*
To remove wet ink stains, cover the stain with salt and leave overnight. Vacuum the following day and the salt should have absorbed the ink. ✹

Lipstick
Remove lipstick stains by rubbing them with petroleum jelly. ✹

Or, rub in some white toothpaste, (not gel), and then wash as normal. ✹

Ink – *on walls*
If your children are particularly fond of leaving you examples of their 'wall-art', try spraying hairspray over the top and then wiping it down with a dry cloth.

Iron Plate - *Stains*
Remove brown stains from your ironing plate by rubbing it, (when cold), with half a cut lemon. ✽

Iron Plate - *Rusty*
Scour the area with salt and beeswax. ✽

Leather
Remove marks from leather by rubbing a bar of moisturising soap with a cloth, and buffing over the affected area. ✽

Lipstick – *on glasses or china*
Lipstick smudges on glassware or chinaware can be hard to remove, even in the dishwasher. This is because the emollients contained within lipstick are designed to stay on your lips – which of course then do a great job at sticking to your glassware and china too!
To make lipstick removal a doddle, gently rub the edges with a little salt, this will lift the lipstick and prime the area for washing. ✽

Liquids – *on carpets*
Most liquid spills can be removed by pouring over mineral or soda water. The bubbles in the treatment will cause the spillage to rise to the surface, making it easier to blot up. ✽

Marble Counters ✽
To remove stubborn stains from marble, gently scour with a paste of bicarbonate of soda and water.

Mattresses

For spills and stains on mattresses, firstly follow the package instructions on upholstery shampoo for tackling mattress stains. Dampen a sponge with warm water and use circular motions to apply the suds. Draw moisture out with a clean, dry towel. Leave as little moisture as possible on the mattress, to avoid mould growth and mildew.

Mud – *on carpets*

A stain you don't have to treat straight away! In fact, you really mustn't treat it straight away! Allow the mud to dry and then brush with a hard bristled brush; vacuum up. ✤

Or, lay slices of raw potato over mud stains in the carpet to help lift them.

Nicotene

Rub or dab with lemon juice to remove nicotine stains. If you have nicotine stained fingers, rub with lemon juice and salt – or lemon juice and a pumice stone. ✤

Paint – *on glass*

Remove paint stains from glass by heating up white distilled vinegar and applying to the area with a cloth. The paint should just wipe off. ✤

Paint – *on wallpaper*

Dry water-based paint can be removed from wallpaper by rubbing the area gently with rubbing alcohol. NB. It is advisable to test an inconspicuous area first, as some inks may fade using this method. ✤

Permanent Ink/Marker – *on carpet*

Douse a cloth with rubbing alcohol and dab on the stain in the carpet. Do not rub. Dab the stain until the ink has lifted. ✤

Permanent Ink/Marker – *on countertops*

Most modern countertops are made of non-permeable materials, so rubbing alcohol, applied directly to the area should dissolve the stain and easily wipe off. ✤

Pollen – *on carpets*
For fresh pollen, remove with clear sticky tape and apply a stain removing product, suitable for carpets.

Red Wine – *on carpets*
For fresh, wet stains, soak with soda water, or white wine, and then pat dry with a dry cloth. ❦

Or, treat with a mixture of white wine and methylated spirits.

Or, sponge with a solution of 1 tablespoon of borax to 1 pint of warm water. ❦

Rust – *on metal*
Rust can be removed by rubbing it with turpentine.

Or, mix equal parts of salt and cream of tartar and moisten with enough water to make a paste. Apply to the stain and leave in direct sunshine, until dry. Repeat if necessary. ❦

Or, make a paste from lemon juice and salt and apply to the affected area. Rub with a dry, soft cloth. ❦

Or, cover rusty tools, gates and other equipment with bicarbonate of soda and then pour over white vinegar, to make the soda bubble. When the solution stops bubbling, scrub it off with a stiff brush. ❦

Scuff Marks – *on vinyl*
Get rid of unsightly scuff marks on your vinyl floor, by taking a tennis shoe or trainer and rubbing the rubber sole over the affected area. The marks should lift off immediately.

Or, spray the marks with a little WD40 and wipe off with kitchen paper towel. This also works for tiled floors.

Shoes – *leather*
Remove grease stains from leather shoes by dabbing them with a little petrol, followed by egg white. Wipe off and buff with a soft cloth.

Shoes – *suede*
Remove grease stains from suede by rubbing them with a cloth dipped in glycerine.

Shoe Polish – *on carpets*
We've all done it – newly polished shoes walked all over the carpet! But don't despair – simply sponge the area with a little dry-cleaning solvent, followed by a solution of 1 teaspoon of mild detergent and 225ml, (1 cup), of luke warm water. Finish by sponging with cold, clean water and pat dry.

Silver
Shine marked and tarnished silver by rubbing it gently with salt.

Or, save the water from cooked potatoes and use it to remove tarnish from silver! Make sure that the water has cooled down and soak a cloth in the liquid. Wipe over the silver and buff dry with a soft cloth. Your silver should be sparkling!

Soot – *on brick*
Give soot-stained brick a clean by making a solution from a can of cola, 110ml, ($\frac{1}{2}$ cup), of your brand of all-purpose household cleaner and 7 pints of water. Mix together in a bucket and sponge over the brickwork. Leave for 20 minutes and then brush the soot stains with a nail brush. Sponge over with fresh water.

Soot – *on carpets*

A tough stain to get rid of – tackle the immediate stain by vacuuming up as much excess as possible. Do not rub – and do not attempt to clean stains with water or detergents. Treat any small residual stains with a solvent cleaner.

Or, vacuum up excess and mix a grease solvent with cornflour or talcum powder to make a paste. Apply a thick layer over the affected area and leave to dry completely. Brush off, then vacuum. Repeat the process if required. ⚘

Standard Stain Remover

For standard stain removal; also suitable for walls and other painted surfaces.

110ml/½ cup of white distilled vinegar
225ml/1 cup of ammonia
¼ cup of baking soda
1 bucket of warm water

Sticky Labels - *general*

Remove sticky labels; or their sticky residue, by spraying a little WD40 or furniture polish onto the area. This should lift the label/glue right off.

Sticky Labels – *on glass*

To remove labels from glass, mirrors, etc – spread on some smooth peanut butter and leave for a few minutes. Wipe off. Repeat the process if necessary. ⚘

Sticky Labels – *on plastic*

Damp a cloth with a little dry-cleaning solution and apply to the label. Leave for 1-2 minutes, just long enough to soak through the label and then wipe off immediately. Wash with soapy water. NB. It is advisable to test a small, inconspicuous area of the item before application.

Strong Scouring Powder *For stains and stubborn grime:-*
16oz/2 cups of bicarbonate of soda
4oz/½ cup of washing powder
Mix together well and store in a clearly labelled, airtight container.

Super-Strong Scouring Powder *For tough stains:-*
8oz/1 cup of bicarbonate of soda
8oz borax
8oz finely powdered pumice or chalk
Mix together well and store in a clearly labelled, airtight container.
NB. This scouring powder should be tested on a small, inconspicuous area before use. Use sparingly.

Suede
Rub suede with glycerine to remove grease spots.

Or, apply talcum powder to the stain and leave overnight. Brush off the next morning. ❧

Tar – *on shoes*
Scrape any residual tar off with a blunt knife or spoon, then blot the area with kitchen paper towel. Moisten an old cloth with methylated spirits and dab the tar stains. Repeat until the tar has lifted. To finish, wash the area with washing up liquid and warm water, followed by cold water.

Timber Floors (without hard finish) – *crayon, gum, candle wax*
Apply ice to break off residual amounts, or iron over an ink blotter or brown paper.

Timber Floors (without hard finish) – *food stains*
Remove with a damp cloth, rub dry with a soft cloth and then wax. ❧

Timber Floors (without hard finish) – *oil & grease*
Rub the area with hydrogen peroxide and cover the stain with cotton. Soak another piece of cotton with ammonia and place over the top of the first piece of cotton. Repeat this process, leave for a few minutes and then remove. Dry the area and buff with a soft cloth.

Urine (Pets) - *on carpets & upholstery*

Pat the area with a cloth, absorbing as much of the urine as possible. Wash the area with washing-up detergent diluted in luke warm water and then rinse with ½ cup of white vinegar, diluted in warm water. ✨

Pat the area with dry towelling and then lay paper kitchen towels, or more towelling over the area and weigh down with heavy books. Leave for 3-4 hours, remove books and towelling and leave to dry.

After clearing up any accidents; negate the nasty-niffs caused by pet urine, by sprinkling the area with a layer of baking soda and leaving it for 20 minutes; vacuum off.

Urine – *on mattresses*
Dab the stain with hydrogen peroxide in a towel, (bearing in mind it will bleach the towel and the mattress). Work from the outside of the stain inwards, this will reduce the risk of the stain spreading.

The hydrogen peroxide will start to bubble, bringing up the stain, blot with a dry cloth. Repeat this process until the stain has been removed.

It is advisable to test an inconspicuous area of the mattress before applying the treatment. You can also use the same method as above but using white vinegar.

After cleaning the stain, neutralise the smell by covering the area with baking soda. Leave overnight and then vacuum the next day.

Vases ❧

Deposits of minerals left by flowers on the interior of vases are difficult to remove. Rub the inside of the vase with salt, then wash with soapy water. If your hand won't fit inside, use a bottle brush with a strong solution of salt and water, or place a handful of uncooked rice inside and shake the contents. Pour out and then wash with soapy water.

Or, stand the vase in warm water with 1 tablespoon of white vinegar and 1 tablespoon of salt. Leave for 3-4 hours, shaking every now and again. ❧

Or, clean the stained insides of a vase by dissolving an Alka-Seltzer tablet in water and leaving for 1 hour. The inside will be sparkling! ❧

Water Marks – *on carpets*
Blot any spills immediately with paper kitchen towel or absorbent cloth; weight down with books to get the maximum amount of absorption.

Water Marks – *on light coloured wooden furniture* ❧
Mix together 1 part white toothpaste, with 1 part bicarbonate of soda and gently rub the mark, in a circular motion, with a soft, damp cloth.

Or, apply mayonnaise to the stain and leave for 8-10 hours. Wipe off with a dry cloth and buff gently. ❧

Water Marks – *on mahogany* ❧
To remove water marks from mahogany, make a paste of coffee granules and a little warm water. Cover the affected area and leave overnight. Polish off with a dry cloth the following day.

Water Marks – *on wood furnishings*
Remove water or heat marks with cream metal polish, by rubbing in the same direction as the grain.

Or, remove white rings left by wet or hot dishes by rubbing the spot with a thin paste of salad oil and salt. Leave for 1-2 hours and wipe off; buff with a dry cloth. ❧

Bathroom

Bathroom

Bathroom Tiles
Clean grubby bathroom tiles with a paste made from bicarbonate of soda and a little bleach. Apply and scrub, then rinse off thoroughly.

Or, apply full strength white vinegar with a sponge and follow with scouring the area with baking soda. Rub with a clean, damp sponge and rinse thoroughly with cold water. ❦

Bubble Bath Residue
Luxurious bath oils can often leave unsightly, grimy tidemarks. To remove stubborn stains, soak a tissue or cotton wool, in white spirit and rub over the area. Leave for an hour or so before rubbing the marks away. Rinse thoroughly.

Copper Stains
Blue-green stains on baths and showers, caused by water with a high copper content can be removed with a paste of equal quantities of cream of tartar and bicarbonate of soda. Rub into the stained areas and leave for 30 minutes; rinse off. Repeat the process if necessary. ❦

Extractor Fans
Remove ingrained dirt from extractor fans with a hot, strong solution of soda crystals. ❦

Floor Tiles
This is a classic old remedy for removing build-up stains from water-based polishes and floor treatments. Make up a bucket of detergent solution, diluted in warm water and mop the area thoroughly. Follow this by moving around the area with a scrubbing brush, to remove the tidemark at the edge of the floor. Stubborn stains can be removed with a wire brush.

Grout
To clean stained grout, place 24oz, (3 cups), of bicarbonate of soda in a bowl and add 225ml, (1 cup), of warm water. Mix into a smooth paste

Grout cont/

and apply to the grout. Scrub with a toothbrush or sponge until stains are removed. Rinse thoroughly and dispose of any excess paste. ❧

Or, soak paper towels in bleach and place them around the grout to get rid of mould and mildew stains, (provided you have adequate ventilation in the room, e.g. an open window). Leave for 1 hour, remove the paper towels and rinse thoroughly.

Hard Water Spots – *on stainless steel*
Remove stubborn hard water spots by soaking a cloth in neat, white vinegar and rubbing the affected area. Rinse with cold water. ❧

Limescale
Limescale and hard water stains can make your kitchen look shabby. To remove stains, apply neat lemon juice to the area and scrub gently with a toothbrush – or for a more abrasive stain remover, add a little salt to the lemon juice. ❧

Or, make a paste from a little borax and white vinegar and apply to the stain. Rinse and clean as normal. ❧

Mildew/Damp Stains – *on walls/ceilings/tiles*
Mix a paste from white vinegar, (or lemon juice), and borax and apply to the area. Leave for 30 minutes, scrub and then rinse thoroughly. ❧

Or, make a solution from salt and lemon juice and rub around the affected area. Rinse off thoroughly. ❧

Mildew – *on shower curtains*
Rub the mildew stains with a paste of baking soda and water. Rinse with cold water. ❧

Mould
For mould-stained shower walls, mix a solution of 1 tablespoon ammonia, 1 tablespoon of vinegar and 200ml warm water. Wipe the walls down and then rinse with cold water; buff dry with a dry cloth.

Mould cont/

Or, moisten a cloth with white vinegar and rub the area. For stubborn stains in tile grout, use a toothbrush to scrub the area. Using vinegar will also prevent new growth. ❧

Porcelain/Enamel Baths & Sinks

Remove stains from your bath by making a paste of cream of tartar, 2 drops of ammonia and diluted hydrogen peroxide. Apply to the bath and leave for 2-2½ hours. Rinse off thoroughly with cold water, followed by a wash with mild, soapy water. Rinse again. NB. Do not use on plastic baths, as this will damage the surface.

Or, rub off stains with cream of tartar sprinkled onto a damp cloth and then rinse. ❧

Or, make a solution using a dilution of one part linseed oil and one part turpentine. Apply to the bath with a soft cloth. Rinse and clean with mild, soapy water, before rinsing again with cold water.

Or, make a solution of 1 part vinegar to 5 parts warm water and rub with a damp cloth. Rinse off with cold water. ❧

Or, mix salt with turpentine to whiten your bathtub and remove stains. Rub away any marks and rinse thoroughly with cold water.

Rust Stains – *around baths*

Remove unsightly rust stains from your bath with a paste made of borax and lemon juice. Start with the borax and add lemon juice a few drops at a time until you have formed a smooth paste. Rub into the stain, then wash off and buff with a soft, dry cloth. ❧

Sealant – *mould, stains* ❧

Sealant around the bath, basin and shower tray can become mouldy and stained. Firstly, clean with a solution of neat white vinegar and then, using a small spatula, wipe over the top with a paste of bicarbonate of soda and a little water. Leave and then wipe off, rinsing well. ❧

Bathroom

33

Shower Stalls

Remove unsightly water spots on your glass/fibreglass shower doors and walls, by rubbing them with car wax. The car wax will work to seal the porous surfaces, which will discourage the development of alkaline deposits. NB. Be careful not to get on the shower floor, as this will make it very slippery.

Soap Scum

Dissolve soap scum with hot white vinegar – keep applying it to the area and scrub until the residue is removed. ❧

Or, mix baking soda with water to make a paste and rub vigorously with a damp sponge. Rinse thoroughly. ❧

Strong Scouring Powder

For stains and stubborn grime:-
16oz/2 cups of bicarbonate of soda
4oz/$\frac{1}{2}$ cup of washing powder

Mix together well and store in a clearly labelled, airtight container.

Super-Strong Scouring Powder

For tough stains:-
8oz/1 cup of bicarbonate of soda
8oz borax
8oz finely powdered pumice or chalk

Mix together well and store in a clearly labelled, airtight container. NB. This scouring powder should be tested on a small, inconspicuous area before use. Use sparingly.

Taps

Remove alkaline water marks from around your taps by soaking paper kitchen towel with white vinegar and wipe around the affected area. Leave for 15 minutes and then scrub the area with a nylon toothbrush and rinse. ❧

Tidemarks

Ugly tidemarks around baths and sinks can be easily removed by applying neat laundry detergent and rinsing with warm water.

Toilets

Mix salt with turpentine to whiten your toilet bowl and remove stains. Rub away any marks with your toilet brush and rinse thoroughly with cold water.

Or, sprinkle the toilet bowl with baking soda and then add vinegar. Give the bowl a good scrub with your toilet brush and rinse with cold water. This will clean and deodorise your toilet bowl at the same time! ✤

Or, drop 2 Alka Seltzer tablets into the toilet bowl and leave for 30 minutes. Brush the bowl with your toilet brush and then flush. ✤

Or, drop a denture tablet down into the toilet bowl and leave overnight. Flush in the morning and your toilet bowl should be sparkling! ✤

Or, naturally and effectively remove stains from your toilet bowl, by pouring in 110ml, ($\frac{1}{2}$ a cup), of white vinegar and leave overnight. Flush in the morning. ✤

NB. If you use bleach in your toilet bowl, do NOT mix bleach with vinegar, ammonia or any other toilet bowl cleaner. Combining bleach with other products and chemicals may produce hazardous toxic gasses.

Toilets – *limescale*

Dissolve limescale stains in toilets by pouring a can of flat cola down into the toilet bowl. Leave for 2-3 hours, then flush. ✤

Or, drop a denture tablet down into the toilet bowl and leave overnight; this cleans the bowl and removes limescale at the same time. Flush in the morning and your toilet bowl should be sparkling! ✤

Watermarks

Get rid of watermarks by applying a limescale remover to the affected area.

Or, apply lemon juice or white vinegar to the area, leave for a while and then rinse off. ⚘

Wash Basins/Sinks

Ugly tidemarks on wash basins/sinks can be easily removed by applying neat laundry detergent and rinsing with warm water.

White Porcelain Sinks

Revitalise stained and yellowed white porcelain sinks by making a solution of 65ml of bicarbonate of soda, 125 ml bleach and 1 litre of warm water. Mix together well and apply to the sink with a sponge. Leave for 10 minutes and then rinse thoroughly. Buff with a dry cloth.

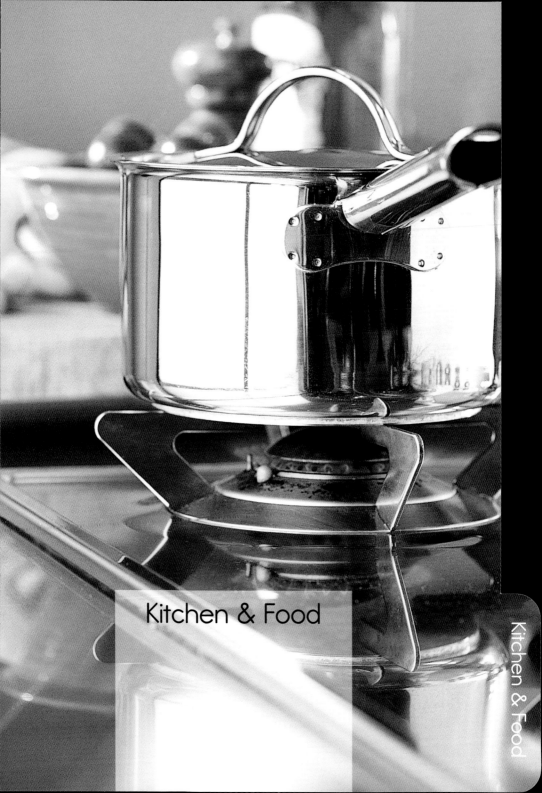

Kitchen & Food

Food & Beverages

Alcohol – *on washable fabric*
Seemingly colourless alcohol such as white wine, vodka, gin etc, can mislead you into thinking that they won't stain, but if left, they will turn brown. For fresh alcohol stains, sponge with warm water; if this doesn't work treat the affected area with glycerine, (for older, dried stains, make sure that you dampen the area first). Rub gently with your fingers, rinse and then wash as normal.

Baby Formula – *on white fabric*
For fresh stains, dampen a clean cloth with water and dip the end in baking soda. Dab the affected area and then wash as normal. ✹

Or, gently rub washing detergent directly into the stain, leave and then rinse. Wash as normal.

Banana – *on washable fabric*
Soak immediately in equal parts of glycerine and water. Remove from the solution and rub with lemon juice. Hang out to dry, preferably in the sun. Wash as normal.

Beer – *on carpets & upholstery*
Take a damp sponge and dab the stain with soda water. ✹

Or, sponge with a mixture of 1 teaspoon of mild detergent and 225ml, (1 cup), of luke warm water, followed by a mixture of 1/3 cup of white wine vinegar in 2/3 cup of water. Finish the process by sponging with cold, clean water.

Beer – *on washable fabric*
Sponge with a mixture of 1 part vinegar to 5 parts water, rinse and then wash in biological washing detergent. Do not use on triacetate fabrics.

Or, gently rub the stain with a mixture of salt and lukewarm water. ✹

Or, apply white vinegar to the stain and rinse off. Wash as normal and then dry in the sun. ✹

Beer – *on wool*
Gently rub the stain with a mixture of salt and tepid water.

Beetroot – *on washable fabric*
Rinse immediately under cold, running water and wash with biological washing detergent.

Berries – *on washable fabric*
Berries can be a nightmare to remove from fabric, but this treatment should work on washable items. Pre-treat any stained items of clothing with your regular stain remover product, then soak the clothing in a solution of 25ml of oxygen bleach to 2 litres of water. Rinse out and wash on the highest temperature that the fabric will take.

Or, for white fabrics, treat with cold water first and soak in chlorinated laundry bleach, if needed. Rinse thoroughly.

Or, cover with a paste of cream of tartar and water and leave for 30 minutes, or until the stain has lifted. Rinse thoroughly.

Or, for tougher stains, sponge with a mixture of equal parts ammonia and methylated spirits. Do not use on triacetate.

Bolognese Sauce – *on washable fabrics*
Remove stubborn Bolognese sauce stains by soaking the fabric in a solution of equal parts glycerine and warm water, (not hot). Wash as normal.

For white fabrics, (but not nylon), soak the fabric in a solution of 1 part hydrogen peroxide to 9 parts cold water. Rinse thoroughly and then wash as normal. Check the fabric care label before soaking.

Butter/Margarine – *for washable fabrics*
Firstly, remove any excess with a spatula or blunt knife and sponge with lukewarm water. Wash in warm, soapy water. For non-washable fabric, sponge with dry-cleaning solution and rinse with cold water.

Butter – *on carpets & upholstery*
Dab with a little dry-cleaning solvent and then sponge with a solution of 1 teaspoon of mild detergent and 225ml, (1 cup), of lukewarm water.

Chewing Gum - *on carpets & upholstery*
Infuriating – but easy to deal with! Place some ice cubes inside a plastic sandwich bag, (or other plastic bag), and press down on the gum for 3-4 minutes. The gum should freeze and come off easily. Dab the area with lemon juice and then wipe off any residue. ❦

Or, rub the gum with smooth peanut butter and it'll miraculously shift! ❦

Or, dab with a little dry-cleaning solvent and then sponge with a solution of 1 teaspoon of mild detergent and 225ml, (1 cup), of lukewarm water.

Chewing Gum - *on washable fabrics*
Place some ice cubes inside a plastic sandwich bag, (or other plastic bag), and press down on the gum for 3-4 minutes. The gum should freeze and come off easily. Dab the area with lemon juice and then wipe off any residue. ❦

Or, using a toothbrush or nailbrush, brush the gum with egg white and leave for 30 minutes. Wash as normal. ❦

Chocolate – *on washable fabric*

Firstly, place the fabric in a plastic bag and place in the fridge for 10 minutes. Remove from the fridge and then scrape off as much excess chocolate as possible with a blunt knife, then sprinkle the area with borax and soak in cold water before washing. ✹

Or, for more stubborn stains, apply a dry-cleaning solvent.

Chocolate – *on carpets*

Sponge with solution of 1 teaspoon of mild detergent and 225ml, (1 cup), of lukewarm water, followed by a solution of 1 tablespoon of ammonia mixed in 110ml, (½ cup), of water. Sponge again with the first solution and finish by sponging with cold, clean water and pat dry.

Coffee & Tea

Get rid of coffee and tea stains in cups and mugs, by rubbing the inside with a damp, clean cloth dipped in bicarbonate of soda, or toothpaste. ✹

Coffee & Tea – *on carpets or upholstery*

Treat fresh stains using a cloth and cold water; blot thoroughly with paper kitchen towel and leave to dry. ✹

For older stains, using a cloth, apply a mixture of liquid detergent mixed with hot water. Rinse with cold water and blot. Leave to dry.

Coffee & Tea – *on countertops*
Rub the surface with a paste of baking soda and a little water. 🌿

Or, for more persistent stains, apply a drop of chlorine bleach to the area and rub until the stain lifts. Wash with hot soapy water, to ensure the bleach is removed, and buff dry.

Coffee – *fresh stains*
Run under the cold tap as soon as possible. If the stain remains, soak in hand-hot liquid detergent.

Or, gently rub with glycerine, using your fingers and rinse with lukewarm water.

Or, soak in a mixture of 1 tablespoon of borax to 225ml, (1 cup), of warm water. 🌿

For more stubborn stains, treat with a solution of half hydrogen peroxide and half water.

Cooking Oil - *on worktops & hobs*
Wipe the residual oil off the area. Mix a solution of 1 part vinegar, 1 part warm water and rub over stain using a damp cloth or sponge. Rinse off with cold water. Suitable for most hobs and worktops. 🌿

Cooking Oil – *on washable fabrics*
Dab with dry-cleaning solvent until the stain lifts.

Or, soak the fabric in water mixed with a little white vinegar. Rinse thoroughly and wash as normal. 🌿

Cream – *on washable fabrics*
Firstly, remove any excess with a spatula or blunt knife and sponge with lukewarm water. Wash in warm, soapy water. For non-washable fabric, sponge with dry-cleaning solution and rinse with cold water.

Curry – *on carpets*
Shift curry stains by applying a mixture of lemon juice and water. 🌿

Curry – *on washable fabrics*
Soak the stain in white spirit, rinse and then wash as normal.

Or, for white or colourfast fabrics, (but not nylon), soak the fabric in a solution of 1 part hydrogen peroxide and 9 parts cold water. Rinse thoroughly and wash as normal.

Egg – *on washable fabrics*
A staple front of t-shirt stain! To remove, scrape away as much as possible and sponge with tepid water. Wash as normal. 🌿

Or, for tougher stains, cover the area with a paste of cream of tartar, a crushed aspirin and water. Leave for 30 minutes, rinse in warm water and wash as normal.

Food Colouring – *on washable fabrics*
Rinse immediately with cool water and wash, adding laundry bleach to the wash cycle. Check the suitability of the fabric first.

Fruit – *on washable fabrics*
Cover fresh stains with a layer of salt, leave for 5 minutes and then wash, without using washing detergent. 🌿

Or, treat with cold water first and soak in chlorinated laundry bleach, if needed. Rinse thoroughly.

Or, cover with a paste of cream of tartar and water and leave for 30 minutes, or until the stain has lifted. Rinse thoroughly. 🌿

Or, for tougher stains, sponge with a mixture of equal parts ammonia and methylated spirits. NB. Do not use on triacetate.

Fruit – *dried on stains/on washable fabrics*
For non-delicates, stretch the fabric over a bowl and pour almost boiling water over the stain. ❧

For delicates, spread the fabric over some absorbent paper kitchen towel and sponge, (on the reverse side to the stain), with hot water. Follow this by dabbing the stain with a little lemon juice and then rinse with hot water. ❧

Fruit Juice - *on washable fabrics*
Soak in a bowl of cold milk for 1-2 hours before washing. ❧

Fruit & Fruit Juice – *on carpets*
Sponge with solution of 1 teaspoon of mild detergent and 225ml, (1 cup), of lukewarm water, followed by a solution of 1 tablespoon of ammonia mixed in 110ml, (½ cup), of water. Sponge again with the first solution and finish by sponging with cold, clean water and pat dry.

Ice Cream – *on carpets*
Sponge with solution of 1 teaspoon of mild detergent and 225ml, (1 cup), of lukewarm water, followed by a solution of 1 tablespoon of ammonia mixed in 110ml, (½ cup), of water. Sponge again with the first solution and finish by sponging with cold, clean water and pat dry.

Ice Cream – *on washable fabrics*
Firstly, remove any excess with a spatula or blunt knife and sponge with lukewarm water. Wash in warm, soapy water. For non-washable fabric, sponge with dry-cleaning solution and rinse with cold water.

Jam – *on washable fabrics*
Mix together a solution of 1 tablespoon of borax, per 1 pint of warm water and soak the stain for 30-45 minutes before washing. ✽

Or, treat the stain with white spirit and rinse with cold water. Wash as normal.

Mayonnaise – *on washable fabrics*
Sponge the affected area with warm water and then soak in washing detergent and warm water. Leave for at least 30 minutes and then wash as normal.

Milk – *on washable fabrics*
Firstly, remove any excess with a spatula or blunt knife and sponge with lukewarm water. Wash in warm, soapy water. For non-washable fabric, sponge with dry-cleaning solution and rinse with cold water.

Pasta Sauce (Tomato) – *on washable fabrics*
Wet the affected area and brush gently with a toothbrush with powdered washing detergent. Rinse and wash as normal.

Red Wine – *on carpet*
Pour on soda water, then pat the area dry. ✽

Red Wine – *on washable fabrics (fresh stain, still wet)*
Soak with soda water and then pat dry with a dry cloth. ✽

Red Wine – *on washable fabrics (older stain)*
Take the item of clothing and gently stretch it over a heatproof bowl. Sprinkle evenly with salt, leave for a few minutes and then pour over hot water, (as hot as the fabric will take, preferably boiling, if possible). ✽

Soft Drinks – *on washable fabrics*
Pre-treat the area with spot stain remover and wash as normal.

Or, sponge the area with equal parts of methylated spirits and water. Rinse and wash as normal.

Food & Beverages

Soft Drinks – *on washable fabrics* **cont/**

For more stubborn stains, pre-treat with glycerine before treating with methylated spirits and water.

Tea – *on washable fabrics (fresh stains)*

Run under the cold tap as soon as possible. If the stain remains, soak in hand-hot liquid detergent.

Or, gently rub with glycerine, using your fingers and rinse with lukewarm water.

Or, soak in a mixture of 1 tablespoon of borax to 225ml, (1 cup), of warm water. ❧

For more stubborn stains, treat with a solution of half hydrogen peroxide and half water.

Tomato Sauce/Ketchup

Remove any excess with a blunt knife or spoon and rinse with cold water. Soak in your normal washing detergent before washing as normal.

White Wine

Treat fresh stains immediately. Soak in cold water with a little ammonia, rinse thoroughly and then wash as normal.

Kitchen

Baby Bottles

Give stained baby bottles a good clean with bicarbonate of soda and hot water. Put a couple of teaspoons of bicarbonate of soda into the bottle and top up with hot water. Leave to soak for 2-3 hours, pour out and rinse thoroughly. ❧

Baked-On Food

Remove food that has been baked onto cooking pans, dishes or plates by lifting the food with a pre-washing treatment of salt. Sprinkle a good layer of salt over the area and dampen. Leave to soak until the salt lifts the baked-on food. Wash with soapy water and rinse. ❧

Burnt Milk – *on pans*

Burnt milk can be a real pain to remove – but not with a little salt! Wet the burned pan and sprinkle salt over the top. Leave to soak in for 20 minutes and then scrub. ❧

Burnt Pans

To remove burned-on food from a pan, let the pan soak in bicarbonate of soda and water for 20-30 minutes before washing. ❧

Or, scrub the pan with bicarbonate of soda and a moist scouring pad. ❧

Or, put $\frac{1}{2}$ cup of baking soda into the pan and fill to $\frac{3}{4}$ full with water. Boil vigorously until all the burnt particles float to the top. Wash as normal. ❧

For a badly burned pan, pour a thick layer of bicarbonate of soda directly onto the bottom of the pan and sprinkle just enough water to moisten the soda. Leave overnight and then scrub clean the following day. ❧

Or, pour a little olive oil into the pan and heat gently. Remove from the heat and leave to stand for 2-3 hours. Pour out and wash the pan as normal. ❧

Casserole/Pie Dishes

If you've got food which has practically welded itself to your casserole dish, (haven't we all at some time or another!), then try filling the dish with boiling water and adding 3 heaped tablespoons of salt, or bicarbonate of soda. Leave for 2 hours, then rinse out and wash as normal. ✿

Or, dip the dish in very hot water and then immediately turn it upside down onto a flat surface. This will trap the steam and make the residue easier to remove. Leave for 1 hour and then wash as normal. ✿

Cast-Iron Pans

To remove build-up in cast-iron pans, cover with a paste of cream of tartar and white vinegar. Leave and then wipe off, any crusting should come off with the paste. Wash as normal. ✿

Coffee Makers – *glass or stainless steel*

Wash stained coffee makers with a solution of 3 tablespoons of bicarbonate of soda to 2 pints of water. Run your coffee maker through its cycle with the soda solution and rinse well. ✿

Or, run full strength vinegar through a normal brew cycle and rinse by running fresh water through the cycle, 2 or 3 times. This will remove any coffee 'sludge' as well as stains. ✿

Coffee & Tea Pots

Give stained coffee and tea pots a new lease of life by pouring in 55g of salt, the juice of 1 lemon, (or white vinegar), and some ice-cubes. Cover with the lid and swish the contents of the pot around for a couple of minutes. Rinse with cold water. ✿

Cooking Oil

Wipe the residual oil off the area. Mix a solution of 1 part vinegar, 1 part warm water and rub over stain using a damp cloth or sponge. Rinse off with cold water. Suitable for most hobs and worktops. ✿

Kitchen

Cutlery

Remove any taint or stains from cutlery by rubbing them with lemon rind. ❦

Or, mix a little salt and lemon juice together and dip in a soft cloth. Rub the cutlery and rinse with warm water. Buff gently with a soft, dry cloth or a chamois. ❦

Dishwashers

Remove food stains and grime from the inside door of your dishwasher by making a paste of 3 parts bicarbonate of soda to 1 part water. ❦

Eggs – *on hard floors*

Make the hassle of having to clear up a dropped, fresh egg easy – cover the spill with salt and leave for 1 minute. The salt will draw the egg together and you'll be able to wipe it up with a sponge or paper towel. ❦

Enamel Pans

Take the strain out of trying to get rid of stains in enamel pans. Soak the pan overnight with salt water; then boil the salt water in the pan the following day. Pour out and rinse with cold water. ❦

Or, finely crush some egg shells and sprinkle some salt inside the pan; rub the inside with a cloth. This will whiten the pan, as well as removing stains. ❦

Extractor Fans

Remove ingrained dirt and grease from extractor fans with a hot, strong solution of soda crystals. ❦

Floor Tiles

This is a classic old remedy for removing a build-up of stains from water-based polishes and floor treatments. Make up a bucket of detergent solution, diluted in warm water and mop the area thoroughly.

Follow this by moving around the area with a scrubbing brush, to remove the tidemark at the edge of the floor. Stubborn stains can be removed with a wire brush.

Glasses
Revive discoloured and stained glasses by making a mixture of a handful of salt to 110ml/½ cup of white vinegar. Soak the glasses overnight and then rinse and wipe clean the following day. ❧

Grill Pans
Banish grease-stained grill pans by firstly scraping off any surface grease with a spatula, or thick paper kitchen towel. Sprinkle the pan with washing soda crystals and then pour in boiling water. Leave to soak for 20-30 minutes, pour out and then wash as normal.

Grout
To clean stained grout, place 24oz, (3 cups), of bicarbonate of soda in a bowl and add 225ml, (1 cup), of warm water. Mix into a smooth paste and apply to the grout. Scrub with a toothbrush or sponge until stains are removed. Rinse thoroughly and dispose of any excess paste. ❧

Or, soak paper towels in bleach and place them around the grout to get rid of mould and mildew stains, (provided you have adequate ventilation in the room, e.g. an open window). Leave for 1 hour, remove the paper towels and rinse thoroughly.

Hard Water Spots – *on stainless steel*
Remove stubborn hard water spots by soaking a cloth in neat, white vinegar and rubbing the affected area. Rinse with cold water. ❧

Kitchen Counters
To remove stubborn stains from marble, formica or plastic kitchen counters, gently scour with a paste of bicarbonate of soda and water. ❧

Kitchen Tiles
Clean grubby, stained kitchen tiles with a paste made from bicarbonate of soda and a little bleach. Apply and scrub, then rinse off thoroughly.

Knives – *rust*
Soak rusty knives in raw linseed oil for 2-3 hours and then wipe off. No more rust! ❧

Limescale

Limescale and hard water stains can make your kitchen look shabby. To remove stains, apply neat lemon juice to the area and scrub gently with a toothbrush – or for a more abrasive stain remover, add a little salt to the lemon juice. ❦

Or, make a paste from a little borax and white vinegar and apply to the stain. Rinse and clean as normal. ❦

Marble Counters

To remove stubborn stains from marble, gently scour with a paste of bicarbonate of soda and water. ❦

Melted Plastic

Have you ever left the bread bag too close to the toaster and ended up with melted plastic stuck all over your toaster? (I think most of us have!) To remove the melted plastic, dampen a cloth and make a mild abrasive with bicarbonate of soda. Gently rub over the affected area and this should remove the plastic… either that or your toaster will look like it's been manufactured by 'Warburton's'! ❦

Microwaves

Remove food stains from inside your microwave by making a paste from bicarbonate of soda and water. Spread over the stained areas and leave. Wipe off and sponge with a clean, damp cloth. ❦

Or, place a bowl filled with water and some bicarbonate of soda inside the microwave and cook on high for about 2 minutes. Remove from the microwave and wipe around the inside of the microwave with a damp sponge or cloth. No scrubbing or soaking required! ❦

Or, place a bowl filled with water and 1 lemon, (cut in quarters), inside the microwave and cook on high for 4-5 minutes. Remove from the microwave and wipe around the inside of the microwave with a damp sponge or cloth. ❦

Non-Stick Pans

Remove grease and oil build-up from non-stick pans by making a solution of 2 tablespoons of bicarbonate of soda, 110ml, and ($\frac{1}{2}$ cup), of vinegar and 225ml, (1 cup), of water. Pour into the pan and bring to the boil; boil for 10-15 minutes and then wash as normal. Be aware of fading on darker colours. ✽

Or, pour a solution of 110ml, ($\frac{1}{2}$ cup), of chlorine bleach, 2 tablespoons of baking soda and 225ml, (1 cup), of water, into the pan and bring to simmering point; simmer for 8-10 minutes. Pour out and wash in soapy water, rinse thoroughly and dry. Be aware of fading on darker colours.

As these solutions can be a little abrasive, it's a good idea to brush the inside with a light coating of cooking oil.

Ovens

For ovens caked with food spills, stains and debris – bicarbonate of soda is a virtual lifesaver! Sprinkle a good layer of bicarbonate of soda over the stained areas and then dampen it, using a spray bottle filled with water. Leave the soda to soak in for 2-3 hours and then wipe with a damp cloth. Repeat the process if necessary. ✽

Ovens & Hobs ✽

If food bubbles over in your oven, or onto your hob, immediately sprinkle a handful of salt over the spill, (before it dries). The salt will negate any odours and the spill will bake into a dry, light crust, which will wipe off easily when the oven, or hob, has cooled.

Rust – *on baking trays* ❧

Sprinkle powdered detergent or baking soda onto metal baking trays which have become rusty. Scour with the cut side of a raw potato. Rinse and dry.

Or, pour cola into the tray and leave overnight. Wash off the following day.

Strong Scouring Powder
For stains and stubborn grime:-

16oz/2 cups of bicarbonate of soda
4oz/½ cup of washing powder

Mix together well and store in a clearly labelled, airtight container.

Super-Strong Scouring Powder
For tough stains:-

8oz/1 cup of bicarbonate of soda
8oz borax
8oz finely powdered pumice or chalk

Mix together well and store in a clearly labelled, airtight container. NB. This scouring powder should be tested on a small, inconspicuous area before use. Use sparingly.

Taps
Remove alkaline water marks from around your taps by soaking paper kitchen towel with white vinegar and wipe around the affected area. Leave for 15 minutes and then scrub the area with a nylon toothbrush and rinse. ❧

Tea/Coffee Stains – *on countertops*
Rub the surface with a paste of baking soda and a little water. ❧

Or, for more persistent stains, apply a drop of chlorine bleach to the area and rub until the stain lifts. Wash with hot soapy water, to ensure the bleach is removed, and buff dry.

Telephone Receivers

Revive stained and grimy telephone receivers by rubbing them with cotton wool dabbed with rubbing alcohol. This will sanitise your phone too!

Thermos Flasks

Bicarbonate of soda is excellent for removing stains from insulated thermoses. Sprinkle bicarbonate of soda into your flask then fill with boiling water, (the amount of soda will depend on the stubbornness of the stain). Put the lid tightly on the thermos and slosh the thermos around! Stains will come off instantly, without any scrubbing.

Tupperware

To remove red staining, apply mustard over the top and leave for 8-10 hours. Wash off with washing-up liquid.

Or, bleach your stained Tupperware containers by placing them in direct sunlight during the summer.

Or, scrub with bicarbonate of soda and a moist scouring pad. Rinse off with warm water.

Washing Machines

Remove grimy stains from the inside door and drum of your washing machine by making a paste of 3 parts bicarbonate of soda to 1 part warm water. Apply the paste to stained areas and then run machine through a rinse cycle to clear residue. ❧

Washing-Up Liquid

Boost your washing-up liquid's stain-removing potential by adding 2 tablespoons of bicarbonate of soda to your washing-up water. ❧

White Porcelain Sinks

Revitalise stained and yellowed white porcelain sinks by making a solution of 65ml of bicarbonate of soda, 125ml bleach and 1 litre of warm water. Mix together well and apply to the sink with a sponge. Leave for 10 minutes and then rinse thoroughly. Buff with a dry cloth. ❧

Laundry
&
Bleach

Laundry & Bleach

Bleaching refers to any chemical or energy source that works to lighten or remove colour, through the process of oxidation.

Bleach & Stain Removal

The most commonly known and used bleaches, are 'chlorine bleaches' and 'oxygen bleaches'. As the process of bleaching removes and fades colour, bleach is a popular agent in the removal of stains. However, despite its obvious benefits in dealing with unwanted stains, it can only be used on certain fabrics and should be used with optimum care. When laundering tough stains, bleaching agents may sometimes be appropriate. But before you add a bleaching agent to your laundry or stain removal remedy, be aware of the differing types and effects:-

Mild Bleaching Agents

for use with all colourfast fabrics

Lemon juice
Hydrogen peroxide
Cream of tartar
Sodium percarbonate
Direct sunlight

Strong Bleaching Agents

for white linen and untreated cotton only

All commercial chlorine-based bleaches

For general laundry purposes, it is advisable to use an oxygen bleach, (such as hydrogen peroxide), as this is a milder chemical and is less likely to damage fabrics.

Guidance for Use
Always read the manufacturers instructions on the container.
In the event of accident, always refer to the care labels and obtain medical advice, where necessary.

+ Never mix bleach with other chemicals, as this can cause the release of lethal gasses

+ Chlorine gas is a respiratory irritant and will burn the skin, therefore when using chlorine bleach always wear protective gloves, goggles and face mask

+ Always ensure when working with bleach that you are in a well ventilated area

+ Limit the amount of time that you work with chlorine bleach, as much as possible

+ All bleaching agents should be rinsed thoroughly from fabrics to avoid damage

+ Begin any bleaching process by using the mildest bleach first, build up to a stronger method if stains have not been removed

+ Only use chlorine bleach if absolutely necessary

+ Always follow the safety instructions on bleaching agents product labels

+ Never use bleach on delicate fabrics, such as silk or wool

+ Always ensure that bleach is appropriately diluted before coming into contact with fabrics

Other Bleaching Agents

Be aware that it will not always be obvious as to what products have a bleaching agent in them. Read the labels of chemicals and products used in the home. Additional chemical names to watch for are:-

Ammonium
Sodium perphosphate
Chlorine dioxide
Zinc peroxide
Benzoyl peroxide
Bromate
Sodium persulfate
Sodium peroxide
Laundry (washable items)

Acids

Acids will damage cloth quickly, so speed is the essence in treating any spillages. Sprinkle the spot immediately with bicarbonate of soda and damp the area with water; the area should start to bubble. Once the bubbling has stopped, rinse the area with warm water.

Or, hold the stain directly over an open bottle of ammonia; the fumes will neutralise the acid and prevent staining. Rinse thoroughly.

Alcohol

Seemingly colourless alcohol such as white wine, vodka, gin etc, can mislead you into thinking that they won't stain, but if left, they will turn brown. For fresh alcohol stains, sponge with warm water; if this doesn't work treat the affected area with glycerine, (for older, dried stains, make sure that you dampen the area first). Rub gently with your fingers, rinse and then wash as normal.

Artificial Nail Glue

Nail glue can be easily removed with acetone, however it is advisable to test an inconspicuous area of the fabric before application. Rinse thoroughly.

Baby Formula – *on white fabric*

For fresh stains, dampen a clean cloth with water and dip the end in baking soda. Dab the affected area and then wash as normal. ✹

Or, gently rub washing detergent directly into the stain, leave and then rinse. Wash as normal.

Baby Oil

Rub some mild liquid dishwashing detergent into the stain and leave for 20 minutes; then wash on 60C, (if the fabric will safely wash at that temperature).

Banana

Soak immediately in equal parts of glycerine and water. Remove from the solution and rub with lemon juice. Hang out to dry, preferably in the sun. Wash as normal.

Battery Acid

Immediately sprinkle baking soda over the area and leave for a few minutes. Sponge the stain with equal parts ammonia and water. Rinse thoroughly and wash on the highest temperature appropriate for the fabric.

Beer

Sponge with a mixture of 1 part vinegar to 5 parts water, rinse and then wash in biological washing detergent. Do not use on triacetate fabrics. ✹

Beer – on wool

Gently rub the stain with a mixture of salt and tepid water. ✹

Beetroot

Rinse immediately under cold, running water and wash with biological washing detergent.

Berries

Berries can be a nightmare to remove from fabric, but this treatment should work on washable items. Pre-treat any stained items of clothing with your regular stain remover product, then soak the clothing in a solution of 25ml of oxygen bleach to 2 litres of water. Rinse out and wash on the highest temperature that the fabric will take.

Or, for white fabrics, treat with cold water first and soak on chlorinated laundry bleach, if needed. Rinse thoroughly.

Or, cover with a paste of cream of tartar and water and leave for 30 minutes, or until the stain has lifted. Rinse thoroughly. ❦

Or, for tougher stains, sponge with a mixture of equal parts ammonia and methylated spirits. Do not use on triacetate.

Bicarbonate of Soda

Soak stained or heavily soiled laundry in bicarbonate of soda prior to washing. This will help lift stains and remove any ingrained smells, (great for stinky football kits!). ❦

Bleach

Water, water and a bit more water! Treat any bleach stains immediately with plenty of cold water. For the treatment of chlorine bleach, soak in a mixture of 1 tablespoon of vinegar to every 600ml of water. Unfortunately, any bleaching that has already occurred will be permanent. ❦

Bleaching

When using bleach to remove stains or whiten your whites, reduce the amount you need to use and boost its performance by adding 4oz of bicarbonate of soda with 4oz bleach, (instead of using 8oz bleach). This will also cut down on the level of bleach odours.

Blood

For fresh blood stains, soak the item of clothing in cold saltwater and then wash in warm, soapy water. For fibres that can take high temperatures, boil after washing. ✿

Or, apply a little diluted hydrogen peroxide to the area, rub and rinse with cold water, (under a tap). Repeat until the stain has lifted.

Or, sponge with diluted ammonia and rinse well.

Butter (& Milk, Cream, Ice-Cream)

Firstly, remove any excess with a spatula or blunt knife and sponge with lukewarm water. Wash in warm, soapy water. For non-washable fabric, sponge with dry-cleaning solution and rinse with cold water.

Bolognese Sauce

Remove stubborn Bolognese sauce stains by soaking the fabric in a solution of equal parts glycerine and warm water, (not hot). Wash as normal.

For white fabrics, (but not nylon), soak the fabric in a solution of 1 part hydrogen peroxide to 9 parts cold water. Rinse thoroughly and then wash as normal. Check the fabric care label before soaking.

Candle Wax

Freeze the item of clothing for 1-2 hours and break off any residual candle wax. Place the garment between two layers brown paper and iron with a warm iron. ❦

If this doesn't get rid of the stain completely, dab with dry-cleaning fluid.

For coloured candle wax, there may be colour staining. To treat, mix together 110ml, ($\frac{1}{2}$ cup), of methylated spirits and 110ml, ($\frac{1}{2}$ cup), of water and sponge gently. Rinse thoroughly.

Canvas Bags

Remove stain marks from canvas bags or hold-alls, by gently brushing the area with a small amount of dry bicarbonate of soda. This will also make them smell fresher! ❦

Chalk

Remove any excess chalk by shaking, or with sticky tape. Apply spot stain remover to the affected area and wash on the highest temperature appropriate for the fabric.

Charcoal – *for colourfast fabrics*

Dab the stain with washing detergent and a few drops of ammonia. Rinse thoroughly and then wash as normal.

Chewing Gum

Infuriating – but easy to deal with! Place some ice cubes inside a plastic sandwich bag, (or other plastic bag), and press down on the gum for 3-4 minutes. The gum should freeze and come off easily. Dab the area with lemon juice and then wipe off any residue. ❦

Or, using a toothbrush or nailbrush, brush the gum with egg white and leave for 30 minutes. Wash as normal. ❦

Chocolate

Firstly, place the fabric in a plastic bag and place in the fridge for 10 minutes. Remove from the fridge and then scrape off as much excess

Chocolate cont/

chocolate as possible with a blunt knife, then sprinkle the area with borax and soak in cold water before washing. ✿

Or, for more stubborn stains, apply a dry-cleaning solvent.

Coffee – *fresh stains*

Run under the cold tap as soon as possible. If the stain remains, soak in hand-hot liquid detergent.

Or, gently rub with glycerine, using your fingers and rinse with lukewarm water.

Or, soak in a mixture of 1 tablespoon of borax to 225ml, (1 cup), of warm water. ✿

For more stubborn stains, treat with a solution of half hydrogen peroxide and half water.

Cooking Oil

Dab with dry-cleaning solvent until the stain lifts.

Or, soak the fabric in water mixed with a little white spirit white vinegar. Rinse thoroughly and wash as normal. ✿

Crayon ✿

If your little ones have ended up with more crayon on their clothes than on the paper, simply add about 8oz of bicarbonate of soda to your wash cycle. The stains should lift out. ✿

Curry

Soak the stain in white spirit, rinse and then wash as normal.

Or, for white or colourfast fabrics, (but not nylon), soak the fabric in a solution of 1 part hydrogen peroxide and 9 parts cold water. Rinse thoroughly and wash as normal.

Deodorant/Antiperspirants

Cover the stains with liquid washing detergent and leave for 10 minutes. Wash as normal.

Or, soak the stain with white vinegar and leave to stand for 30-45 minutes. Wash in the washing machine, on the hottest temperature that the garment can be safely washed in. ✤

Or, use chlorinated laundry bleach in your wash cycle.

Egg

A staple front of t-shirt stain! To remove, scrape away as much as possible and sponge with tepid water. Wash as normal. ✤

Or, for tougher stains, cover the area with a paste of cream of tartar, a crushed aspirin and water. Leave for 30 minutes, rinse in warm water and wash as normal. ✤

Face Cloths

Remove soapy residue stains from face cloths before washing, by soaking them in a solution of white vinegar and water. ✤

Felt-Tip Pen

If you have kids, you will have felt-tip pen stains! Use hard soap and rub well into the stain to lubricate, and wash as normal. Particularly stubborn stains can be treated with a dab of methylated spirits and then washed again to remove any final traces. ✤

Food Colouring

Rinse immediately with cool water and wash, adding laundry bleach to the wash cycle.

Foundation - *make-up*

Scrape off any excess and soak for 5 minutes, in a solution of 5ml ammonia to 500ml of warm water. Rinse thoroughly and wash on the highest temperature appropriate to the fabric.

Fruit

Cover fresh stains with a layer of salt, leave for 5 minutes and then wash, without using washing detergent. 🌱

Or, treat with cold water first and soak in chlorinated laundry bleach, if needed. Rinse thoroughly.

Or, cover with a paste of cream of tartar and water and leave for 30 minutes, or until the stain has lifted. Rinse thoroughly. 🌱

Or, for tougher stains, sponge with a mixture of equal parts ammonia and methylated spirits. NB. Do not use on triacetate.

Fruit – *dried on stains*

For non-delicates, stretch the fabric over a bowl and pour almost boiling water over the stain. 🌱

For delicates, spread the fabric over some absorbent paper kitchen towel and sponge, (on the reverse side to the stain), with hot water. Follow this by dabbing the stain with a little lemon juice and then rinse with hot water. 🌱

Fruit Juice

Soak in a bowl of cold milk for 1-2 hours before washing. 🌱

Glue (PVA)

Dab the stain with methylated spirit and rinse with cold water before washing.

Or, place a few drops of eucalyptus oil on the stain and leave for 2-3 minutes before washing.

Repeat if necessary. Finish with a dab of methylated spirits if the stain has not already completely gone.

Grass Stains

Sponge the stain with rubbing alcohol and leave to dry naturally. Rinse and then work a little washing detergent into the stain. Rinse and dry naturally. Wash as normal. Not for use on delicate fabrics.

Or, soak the fabric in a solution of white vinegar and warm water for 1-2 hours. Rinse and wash as normal. 🌿

Or, make a paste from equal parts of salt and cream of tartar, (with water), and gently rub the stain. Wash and dry in the sun. 🌿

Or, dab the stain with methylated spirit and rinse with cold water before washing.

For more stubborn stains, soak in a solution of chlorinated laundry bleach and then rinse well before washing as normal.

Or, dab the stain with hydrogen peroxide and rinse with cold water before washing.

Grease – *fresh stains*

Apply a thick layer of talcum powder to the stain and leave for 8-10 hours. Brush off and wash as normal. 🌿

Or, iron the garment between two layers of blotting paper, or brown paper. The grease should lift through the paper, leaving a mark on it. 🌿

Or, if you're out and about and unable to deal with the grease spot straight away, sprinkle salt over the area in order to absorb the grease. When you get home, rub the area with neat detergent and wash as normal. 🌿

Or, mix 1 part salt to 4 parts alcohol and rub on the stain, then wash as normal.

Grease – *on suede*
Dip a toothbrush in white vinegar and gently brush the stain. ❧

Hair Dye
Soak immediately in cold water, leave for 30 minutes. Gently rub the stain with neat washing-up detergent and sponge off with cold water. Wash as normal.

If the stain persists, do not dry – soak in warm water with biological detergent and leave for 8-10 hours. Rinse and wash as normal.

Handkerchiefs
Soak stained handkerchiefs in a solution of salt water before washing. ❧

Ink
Dip a cotton bud, (Q-tip), with eau-de-cologne and apply to the stain. Repeat until the stain lifts and then wash as normal.

Or, dab alcohol or methylated spirits on the stain and leave for 30 minutes before washing.

Ink – *ballpoint pen*
Place the fabric on top of absorbent paper kitchen towel and spray the stain with alcohol-based hair spray. Leave to soak for a few minutes and then blot with a dry cloth. Repeat until the stain has lifted. It is advisable to test an inconspicuous area of the fabric before application.

Iodine
Fresh stains can be sponged with water, washed as normal and placed in the sun to dry.

Ironing & Stains – *CAUTION*
Don't be tempted to freshen up dirty clothes with a quick rub over with the iron – the heat will set any stains into the fabric and make them virtually impossible to remove.

Jam

Mix together a solution of 1 tablespoon of borax, per 1 pint of warm water and soak the stain for 30-45 minutes before washing. 🌿

Or, treat the stain with white spirit and rinse with cold water. Wash as normal.

Lipstick

Dab the stain with rubbing alcohol, followed by a little washing-up detergent. Wash as normal. 🌿

Or, spray a little hairspray on the stain and leave for 3-4 minutes. Wipe off with a clean cloth and wash as normal.

Or, remove lipstick stains by rubbing them with petroleum jelly. 🌿

Or, rub in some white toothpaste, (not gel), and then wash as normal. 🌿

Make-Up

Pre-treat with your usual stain-removing product and then wash as normal.

For more stubborn stains, dab on a little dry-cleaning solvent, followed by a mixture of diluted washing detergent and 2 drops of ammonia. Rinse thoroughly and wash as normal.

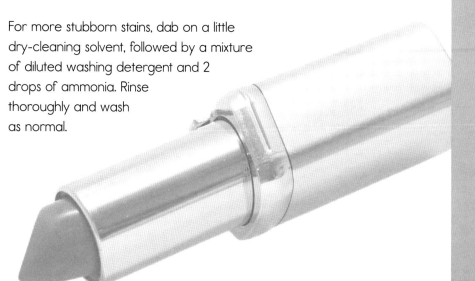

Mascara

Gently rub neat liquid detergent into the stain and rinse. Wash as normal.

Or, treat with a spot stain remover and then wash as normal.

Mayonnaise

Sponge the affected area with warm water and then soak in washing detergent and warm water. Leave for at least 30 minutes and then wash as normal.

Mildew – *on clothes*

Treat mildew immediately, before it has time to damage the fabric. Remove loose particles by brushing or shaking the garment. Pre-soak in cold water and then wash in hot water, with a strong detergent. Laundry bleach can be added to whites - vinegar added to the final rinse of your wash cycle will get rid of any smell of bleach from the fabric.

Milk/Cream/Butter

Dab with cold water first, then iron between two layers of blotting paper to remove the grease/fat. ✲

Mould

Add ½ teaspoon of tea tree oil to your laundry cycle for towels and other fabrics which are prone to mould. ✲

Mud

Brush off any excess dried mud and wash on the highest temperature appropriate to the fabric care instructions. ✲

Or, brush off any excess and dab any stains with dry-cleaning solution, followed by a little white spirit. Wash in a bowl with normal washing detergent and rinse with cold water.

Or, pre-treat with a spot stain remover and wash as normal.

For more stubborn stains, soak in washing detergent overnight and wash the following day.

Or, make a paste from ammonia and a mild powder detergent and apply to the stain. Leave for 10 minutes and then wash on the highest temperature appropriate for the fabric. NB. Spot testing advised.

Newspaper Print
Sponge the area with methylated spirit, rinse thoroughly and then wash as normal.

Nail Polish
Apply acetone or amyl acetate to the stain, but be wary of what fabric you apply this to, as these chemicals will dissolve some fabrics. Wash as normal.

If there is still a colour stain in the fabric, white cottons and linens can be treated by using laundry bleach in your wash cycle.

Nappies
Budge stubborn stains off your toweling nappies, by soaking them in water with a tablespoon of bicarbonate of soda. Wash as normal and then hang out in direct sunshine, so that the sun can do the rest of the job by fading any residual stains. ❧

Oil & Grease
Add 4oz of bicarbonate of soda to your washing machine cycle, this will assist in breaking down oil and grease stains. ❧

Oil & Grease – *light oils*
For 'light' oils, such as baby oil, hair oil, etc; rub some washing-up detergent into the stain and leave for 15-20 minutes. Hot wash the clothing, (60C-65C), as long as the fabric will not be damaged by the heat.

Oil & Grease – *heavy oils*
For heavier oils, such as motor grease and oils, begin by scraping away as much excess oil as possible. Rub Vaseline into the fabric and wash in a good quality laundry detergent.

Or, for dried oil or grease, treat with a spot stain remover and launder using a good quality laundry detergent.

Paint (Oil-Based)

Scrape off as much as possible, then treat with amyl acetate. Wash as normal.

Or, treat stains whilst wet, using white spirit. Dab the stain until the paint has lifted and then wash in a good quality detergent. You may have to wash the item more than once to remove the odour.

Paint (Water-Based)

Treat any stains whilst they are still fresh and wet by rinsing with cold water. Dab any residual stains with methylated spirits, (if the fabric allows). Avoid allowing the stain to dry, because when dried, these paint stains will almost certainly not come out.

Pasta Sauce

Wet the affected area and brush gently with a toothbrush with powdered washing detergent. Rinse and wash as normal.

Pencil Marks – *lead*

Treat with a spot stain remover and wash as normal. For un-washable fabrics, try rubbing with a rubber eraser, (really!).

Perfume

Wet the stain and dab the stain with glycerine. Rinse out thoroughly and then wash as normal.

Perspiration

Sponge stains with white vinegar and rinse with cold water. For wool garments, sponge with a solution of 1 part lemon juice and 1 part water. 🌿

Or, dissolve 4 tablespoons of salt in 1 litre of hot water, then sponge the area with the mixture until the stain lifts. 🌿

Or, soak overnight in a mixture of equal parts of ammonia and water, with a little washing-up detergent. Wash as normal.

Pollen

For fresh pollen, remove with clear sticky tape and then wash as normal. For more stubborn stains, use a stain remover product before washing.

Quilted or Down Jackets

Spot-clean stains or grime on cuffs, firstly checking for weak seams, then hand wash gently and rinse well. Put knotted towels or tennis balls with the jacket inside the tumble dryer and dry until the lining fluffs up. Air outdoors, if possible.

Red Wine – *fresh stains, still wet*

Soak with soda water, or white wine, and then soak in cold water with a little ammonia. Rinse thoroughly and wash as normal.

Or, sponge with a solution of 1 tablespoon of borax to 1 pint of warm water. 🌿

Red Wine – *older stains*

Take the item of clothing and gently stretch it over a heatproof bowl. Sprinkle evenly with salt, or borax, leave for a few minutes and then pour over hot water. 🌿

Red wine can be a real pain to remove, so if spilling red wine is a regular occurrence, you might want to invest in a specialist cleaning product specifically targeting such stains. Either that, or change your choice of drink!

Rust – *on white cotton*
Treat rust stains with the juice of 1 lemon mixed with 1 tablespoon of salt. Rub the stain well, wash as normal and dry in the sun. You may need to repeat this process more than once to lift the stain completely. ❧

Or, add 225ml, (1 cup), of lemon juice to the wash cycle. It'll zap the stains and make your laundry smell gorgeously fresh! ❧

Or, make a paste of equal parts of cream of tartar and salt, (with water), and apply to the stain. Rinse out and dry in the sun. ❧

Or, soak for 3-4 hours in water that has been used to boil white rice, before washing. ❧

Running Colours – *on white cotton or linen*
The bane of many a household – that rogue coloured sock that has mysteriously found its way into the white wash; and now everything's pink or grey! Use chlorinated laundry bleach in your wash cycle to get your items back to their former glory.

Running Colours – *on silk, wool & delicates*
Treat with diluted hydrogen peroxide and rinse thoroughly before washing as normal.

Scorch Marks
Dab the affected area with 1 part glycerine and 2 parts water and rub in, using your fingers. Soak in a solution of 50g borax with 600ml of warm water for 20 minutes. Rinse thoroughly and dry.

Shirt Collars & Cuffs
Clean grubby collars and cuffs by brushing then with your normal shampoo before washing them.

Shoe Polish
Scrape off any excess polish and then treat with glycerine, by pouring onto the fabric and rubbing it lightly with your fingers. Leave for 30 minutes and then rinse with warm water.

Shoe Polish cont/

Or, dab on a little dry-cleaning solvent, followed by a mixture of diluted washing detergent and 2 drops of ammonia. Rinse thoroughly and wash as normal. If there is still residual staining, treat with a little white spirit, rinse and wash.

Soft Drinks

Pre-treat the area with spot stain remover and wash as normal.

Or, sponge the area with equal parts of methylated spirits and water. Rinse and wash as normal.

For more stubborn stains, pre-treat with glycerine before treating with methylated spirits and water.

Tar

Scrape off what you can and then apply a few drops of eucalyptus oil on the stain and leave for 2-3 minutes before washing. Repeat if necessary. Finish with a dab of methylated spirits if the stain has not already completely gone. 🌿

Or, apply white toothpaste to the stain, (not gel), and leave for a while. Wash as normal. 🌿

Tea – *fresh stains*

Run under the cold tap as soon as possible. If the stain remains, soak in hand-hot liquid detergent.

Or, gently rub with glycerine, using your fingers and rinse with lukewarm water.

Or, soak in a mixture of 1 tablespoon of borax to 225ml, (1 cup), of warm water. 🌿

For more stubborn stains, treat with a solution of half hydrogen peroxide and half water.

Tea Towels

Eradicate stains from your tea towels by putting a few slices of lemon into a saucepan of water and adding the tea towels. Boil for 15-20 minutes and then add to a normal wash cycle. ✿

Ties

Trying to remove a stain from a tie can result in a water mark, which looks just as bad as the original stain! Blot away any excess stains with a clean cloth and take it to the dry cleaner, as soon as possible. Stains set within 24-48 hours, so don't delay. Don't attempt to rub the stain or you could end up rubbing colour from the fabric, especially if it's silk. This is a stain that should be left to the professionals!

Tobacco

Rinse the stain with cold water and soak with white vinegar. Rinse out and wash as normal. ✿

Or, pour glycerine over the stain and rub gently between your fingers. Leave for 30 minutes and then wash as normal.

Tomato Sauce/Ketchup

Remove any excess with a blunt knife or spoon and rinse with cold water. Soak in your normal washing detergent before washing as normal.

Urine

Accidents will happen where kids are concerned, so knowing how to treat urine stains is a must. For fresh stains, rinse immediately with cold, running water and wash in biological washing detergent.

Or, try soaking the stain in equal parts of white vinegar and water, rinse and wash as normal. ✸

For more stubborn stains, sponge the stain with a diluted hydrogen peroxide and rinse with warm water. Wash as normal. Or, soak the garment in a weak solution of hydrogen peroxide and water for 4-5 hours. Rinse and wash in a biological washing detergent.

Banish the smell of urine by adding a can of cola to your wash cycle. ✸

Vomit

The quicker you can deal with these stains, the better. You are, of course, at the mercy of what has been eaten – so speed is definitely the key. Use a spoon to remove as much excess vomit as you can and then rinse the stain with cold water. For washable clothing, wash immediately in a biological washing detergent. For carpets and upholstery, sponge the area with a solution of borax and warm water. Rinse thoroughly, dabbing and then blotting up the moisture – do not rub. Repeat as necessary.

If you know what's been consumed, you can treat the stain with a stain-appropriate solution, e.g. if you have a red wine stain on clothing after vomiting, soak the item of clothing in salt water before washing.

Or, for clothing, damp the affected area and sprinkle over a layer of pepsin powder. Leave for 30-35 minutes and then rinse. Wash as normal.

Or, for smaller stains, sponge the area with a little ammonia, diluted in warm water.

To rid carpets and upholstery of the unpleasant smells created by vomit, sprinkle baking soda over the area and leave for 1-2 hours before vacuuming off. ✸

Water Marks

Remove water marks in clothing by holding the area in the steam of a boiling kettle. Leave long enough to just damp the area and rub with a dry piece of the same material. 🌿

White Wine

Treat fresh stains immediately. Soak in cold water with a little ammonia, rinse thoroughly and then wash as normal.

White Cotton & Linen

Brighten discoloured and yellow items by soaking them for 1 hour in a salt and baking soda solution. 🌿

Outside, DIY
& Pets

Outside, DIY & Pets

Outdoor & DIY

Bird Droppings
They look and sound charming up in the trees, but birds can be a bit of a pest when they choose you as their unsuspecting target! Scrape off any excess droppings and sponge the area with a solution of borax and warm water. ✺

If the stain persists, soak in diluted chorine bleach, (for white cottons and linen), or diluted hydrogen peroxide, (for coloured items and synthetics, except nylon).

Garden Furniture – *resin stains*
Clean resin off patio and other garden furniture by mixing 1 part detergent to 8 parts bleach. Wipe onto furniture and leave for 30 minutes. Rinse off and repeat if necessary. Keep children and pets well away from the area.

Glue – *table & chair joints*

Whilst repairing or renovating tables and chairs, loosen and remove old glue from rungs and joints by applying full strength white vinegar directly to the affected area. �><

Grass Stains

The bane of parents and sports enthusiasts everywhere! Sponge the stain with rubbing alcohol and leave to dry naturally. Rinse and then work a little washing detergent into the stain. Rinse and dry naurally. Wash as normal. Not for use on delicate fabrics.

Or, soak the fabric in a solution of white vinegar and warm water for 1-2 hours. Rinse and wash as normal. �><

Or, make a paste from equal parts of salt and cream of tartar, (with water), and gently rub the stain. Wash and dry in the sun. �><

Or, dab the stain with methylated spirit and rinse with cold water before washing.

For more stubborn stains, soak in a solution of chlorinated laundry bleach and then rinse well before washing as normal.

Or, dab the stain with hydrogen peroxide and rinse with cold water before washing.

Grease/Oil – *on concrete*

Sprinkle the affected area with dry cement, or cat litter, and leave it to absorb the grease. Once the liquid has drawn up and the absorbent material has 'clumped', brush up with a hard bristled brush.

Grease – *from hands*

After a particulary dirty job working with grease, apply a little WD40 to your hands and rub together. Wipe with paper kitchen towel and then wash immediately with soap and water.

Paint – *from glass*
Remove paint stains from glass by heating up white distilled vinegar and applying to the area with a cloth. The paint should just wipe off. 🌿

Paint – *from wallpaper*
Dry water-based paint can be removed from wallpaper by rubbing the area gently with rubbing alcohol. NB. It is advisable to test an inconspicuous area first, as some inks may fade using this method.

Or, spray the area with methylated spirits. Leave and then rinse off.

Rusty Tools
Clean up those old tools by soaking them in full strength white distilled vinegar for several days. Rust, grime and dirt should all be removed. ✣

Wooden Decking – *mildew*
Make a solution of 1 cup of ammonia, ½ cup of white vinegar and ½ cup of baking soda, mixed with 7 pints of water. Use a bristle brush or broom dipped in the solution and brush onto the deck to remove troublesome mildew.

Wooden Decking – *oil stains*
Remove oils stains, (such as baby oil, sun tan lotion, etc), from decking by sprinkling baking soda liberally on the area; leave for 1-2 hours for the soda to absorb the oil, (the soda should turn yellow), and then sweep away with a brush. Repeat if necessary. ✣

Pets

Dog Collars

Scrub grease, grime and other stains off your dog's collar by using a solution of baking soda dissolved in hot water. Soak nylon collars in a solution of equal parts of baking soda and vinegar in hot water. The collar will soak clean in 20-30 minutes; rinse well and hang out to dry. ✤

Vomit

The quicker you can deal with these stains, the better. You are, of course, at the mercy of what your pet has eaten – so speed is definitely the key. Use a spoon to remove as much excess vomit as you can and then rinse the stain with cold water. For washable clothing, wash immediately in a biological washing detergent. For carpets and upholstery, sponge the area with a solution of borax and warm water. Rinse thoroughly, dabbing and then blotting up the moisture. Repeat as necessary.

To rid carpets and upholstery of the unpleasant smells created by vomit, sprinkle baking soda over the area and leave for 30 minutes before vacuuming off. ✤

Urine (Pets) – *on carpets & upholstery*

Treat immediately to limit seepage. Pat the area with a cloth, absorbing as much of the urine as possible. Wash the area with washing-up detergent diluted in lukewarm water and then rinse with ½ cup of white vinegar, diluted in warm water. Pat the area with dry toweling and then lay paper kitchen towels, or more toweling over the area and weigh down with heavy books. Leave for 3-4 hours, remove books and toweling and leave to dry. ✤

Or, absorb as much urine as possible and treat the area immediately with soda water, to minimise staining. Follow this up by sponging the stain with some salt water. Rinse with cold water and blot dry.

After clearing up any accidents; negate the nasty-niffs, by sprinkling the area with a layer of baking soda and leaving it for 30 minutes; vacuum off.

Pet Urine – *on concrete*
Get rid of stains and the unpleasant smell of pet urine from concrete, by scrubbing the area with a solution of half white vinegar and half water. ✿

NB. Never use an ammonia-based solution to treat urine stains, as this will practically invite your pet back to pee in the same spot!

Or, spray the area with methylated spirits. Leave and then rinse off.

Urine – *on washable fabrics*
For fresh stains, rinse immediately with cold, running water and wash in biological washing detergent.

For older stains, soak the garment in a weak solution of hydrogen peroxide and water for 4-5 hours. Rinse and wash in a biological washing detergent.

Faeces – *on carpets & upholstery*
Although pretty revolting to have to deal with, it's also quite easy to remove. Use a spoon to remove as much excess as you can and then rinse the stain with cold water. Sponge the area with a solution of borax and warm water. Rinse thoroughly, dabbing and then blotting up the moisture. Repeat as necessary. ✿

Faeces – *on washable fabric*
Use a spoon to remove as much excess as you can and then rinse the stain with cold water. Soak in a biological washing detergent and warm water, or borax and warm water. Rinse and then wash as normal, using a biological washing detergent.

Pets

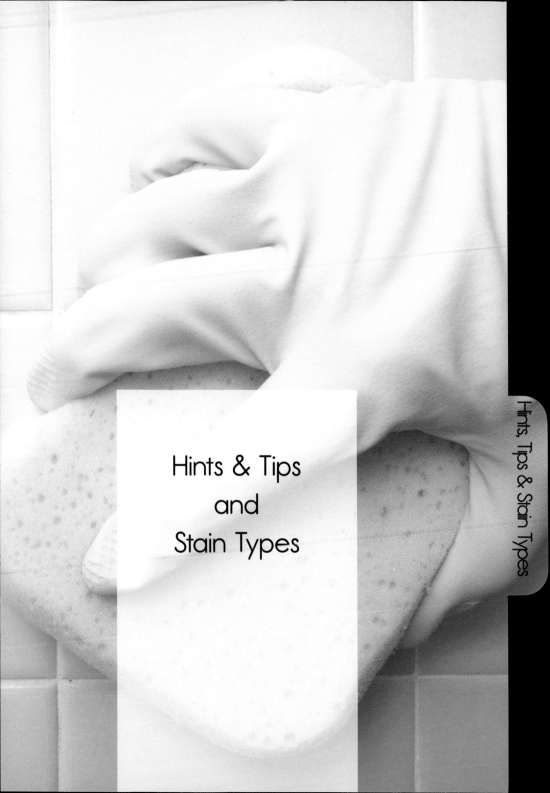

Hints & Tips
and
Stain Types

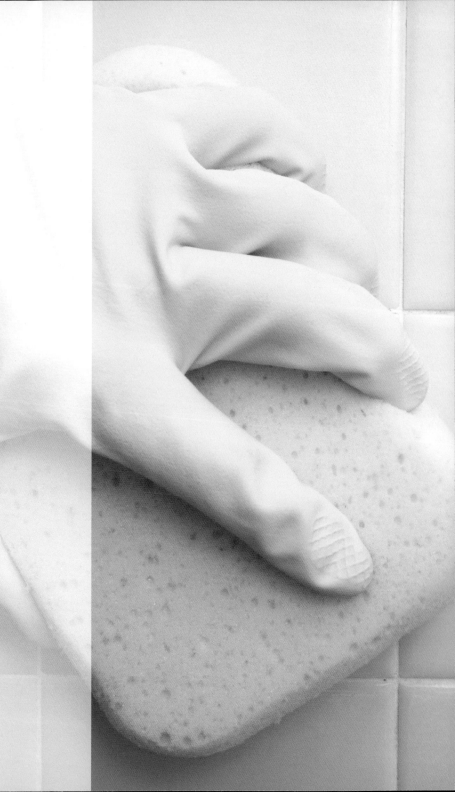

Stain Removing Hints & Tips

Act Fast!
Speed is the essence in successfully dealing with stains – the longer a spillage is left, the greater chance that the stain will set and be permanent. Most stains can be easily lifted whilst still fresh, but become a nightmare once they've been allowed to soak in or dry. So, it might be a pain having to break from your quiet time to mop up your coffee spill, or leave the fun of your party guests to deal with the split red wine stain – but you'll be grateful that you did afterwards.

Be Prepared!
In order to treat stains effectively, you have to catch them as soon as they occur – that means being prepared! Rather than have an excess amount of products and chemicals in your house, invest in keeping in white vinegar, lemons, salt and baking soda; along with a spot stain removal product and/or bleach. This will stand you in good stead to at least be able to initially treat stains, before you get chance to purchase the appropriate chemical or product for the stain-type. Or, if you have a regular stain-type in your house, (e.g. ink, crayon, milk, etc), then keep in what tackles that stain the most effectively.

Care Labels
Always check the care labels on garments prior to using any stain removal products or remedies.

Days Out
Be prepared, (not to mention smug!), by taking a stain removal stick out with you for days out – especially useful if you have kids!

Don't Panic!
We've all been there – you've got 5 minutes in which to feed your toddler, get yourself and them dressed, put the washing out, feed the cat and get out the house – and suddenly you spill coffee all over your beige carpet. Aaargghhh!!!! Negotiating world peace would be a more attractive challenge at this precise moment. But whatever you do – don't panic and treat the stain with the nearest available product or wet cloth; you could

Don't Panic! cont/

make it much worse. Calmly dealing with a potentially permanent stain is definitely the key to success. So, count to 20, take a deep breath and work the stain as though you've all the time in the world – or at least 15 minutes anyway.

Don't Rub

Whatever you do – don't rub stains! No matter how tempting it may be, or whether you think you know better. Rubbing simply pushes the stain further into the fabric and makes it harder to remove, if not impossible.

Dried Stains

Dried stains will be significantly more difficult to remove – if not impossible. Wherever possible, treat the stain whilst fresh, damp or wet.

Dry-Clean Only Fabrics

For fabrics that are dry-clean only, it's advisable not to work on the stain too much, but simply to blot or scrape away any excess. Take the item to your professional cleaners as soon as possible.

Gently Does It

Use milder methods of stain removal first – there's no point in bringing out the big-boy stain removers, if all you need is something like a little water and baking soda. It's less damaging to your fabrics and household surfaces – and certainly kinder to your body and the environment.

Identify It!

Arguably the most important step of any stain removal process; before you treat any stain – make sure that you identify it! You could inadvertently end up making the stain worse and/or permanent by treating it with the wrong product or chemical.

If you really don't know what the stain is, try to take an informed guess what type of stain it falls under by closely examining it first. Ask yourself things such as; what does it smell like? Is it food or drink? Is it paint, ink or some other chemical? What does it feel like? Is it greasy? Is it soaked into the fabric? Once you've a clearer idea, you can go ahead and treat the stain. Refer to the 'Stain Types' section contained in this book for more pointers.

Ironing & Stains

Don't be tempted to freshen up dirty clothes with a quick rub over with the iron – the heat will set any stains into the fabric and make them virtually impossible to remove.

Mixing Cleaning Solutions

Be very careful about which cleaners you use together and do not mix products without knowing the potential effects. Mixing solutions can emit fumes which can be harmful – and potentially fatal. Chlorine bleach and ammonia are an especially dangerous combination.

Persistent Stains

If a stain has not been removed, despite using a stain removal remedy and washing, try another stain removal method before heat drying the item. Once the item has been heat dried, it may become impossible to remove the stain altogether.

Rinsing

Always rinse well between applications of different cleaning solutions and/or before use.

Soaking

When soaking fabrics, make sure that they are properly immersed, otherwise you may find yourself having to tackle water mark stains. To optimise immersion, squeeze out the air from the fabric and weigh down with a couple of bottles of water.

Spot Test

It's advisable to test stain removal products and methods on an inconspicuous area, if at all possible. Some stain removers and solvents will be more abrasive and harsh than others and may cause more damage than the original stain.

So unless you're certain about the affect it will have, opt for testing first. For clothes, try testing under the hemline before moving to the site of the stain.

To Wash or Not To Wash?

Don't just automatically assume that the fabric is washable – you'll get a nasty shock in the shape and size of a toddler's item of clothing, if you unwittingly put in your best, (dry-clean only), jumper! Check your care labels thoroughly.

Washable Stains – *First Action - Fluid*

Blot the liquid with kitchen paper towels or a dry cloth

Washable Stains – *First Action - Food*

Use a blunt knife, spatula or spoon to scrape off any residual food before soaking.

Working Stains

Always work from the outside of the stain, inwards. This will help to minimise the spread of the stain.

Stain Types

Stains, at their most basic level, are any discoloration or mark which differs from the material or surface from which it is on. There are literally hundreds of different stains – in fact any substance that can spill, drop, burn, fester or bleach, can cause a stain. But despite there being so many possible variations of stains, it is possible to group them into 'types' which can help to determine how to treat an unidentified, or particular type of stain. The following stain types and examples provide standard removal methods for washable fabrics only.

Protein Stains	**Tannin Stains**
Soak in cold water, then wash as normal in warm water. If the stain is persistent, soak again for a further 30-40 minutes and then wash again. Mild bleaching may be necessary to remove food colours.	Treat stains with detergent and hot water, do not use soaps bars or flakes.
	Older or more stubborn stains may need bleaching.
Baby food	Alcohol
Baby formula	Beer
Blood	Berries
Cheese/sauces	Coffee
Cream	Felt-tip pen
Egg	Fruit juice
Gelatin	Perfume
Ice cream	Tea
Milk	Tomato juice/ketchup
Mud	
PVA glue	
Urine	
Vomit	

Oil-Based Stains

Treat oil-based stains by using a heavy-duty detergent in hot water for soaking, then wash as normal. Repeat the process, if necessary. Pretreatment stain removal products, especially for oil-based stains will also be effective.

Bacon fat
Butter/margarine
Cooking fats & oils
Cosmetic creams (hand & face lotions)
Lard
Mayonnaise
Motor oil
Suntan oil/lotion

Dye Stains

Treat dye stains by using a heavy-duty liquid detergent wash only. Pre-treat the stain with the liquid detergent and then rinse thoroughly.

Bleaching may be required, if the fabric is suitable for bleaching agents.

Cherry juice
Colour bleeding
Coloured drinks
Grass
Ink
Mustard
Paint

Index and
Conversions

Index & Conversions

index

A - C	90
C - G	91
H - M	92
N - R	93
S - T	94
U - W	95
Conversions	96

A

Acetone pp.5
Acids pp.57
Alcohol pp.57
Alcohol Spots, wooden furniture pp.15
Alcohol, washable fabric pp.37
Ammonia (household) pp.5
Artificial Nail Glue pp.57

B

Baby Bottles pp.46
Baby Formula pp.58
Baby Formula, white fabric pp.37
Baby Oil pp.58
Baked on Food pp.46
Baking soda pp.8
Banana pp.58
Banana, washable fabric pp.37
Bathroom Tiles pp.31
Battery Acid pp.58
Beer pp.58
Beer, carpets & upholstery pp.15, pp.37
Beer, washable fabric pp.37
Beer, wool pp.38, pp.58
Beeswax pp.9
Beetroot pp.59
Beetroot, washable fabric pp.38
Berries pp.59
Berries, washable fabric pp.38
Bicarbonate of Soda pp.59
Bird Droppings pp.77
Bleach & Stain Removal pp.55
Bleach pp.59
Bleach, guidance for use pp.56

Bleaching Agents (others) pp.57
Bleaching pp.59
Blinds, fabric pp.15
Blood pp.60
Blood, carpets & upholstery pp.15
Blood, mattresses pp.15
Bolognese Sauce pp.60
Bolognese Sauce, washable fabric pp.39
Books pp.15
Borax pp.9
Bubble Bath Residue pp.31
Burnt Milk pp.46
Burnt Pans pp.46
Butter (& Milk, Cream, Ice Cream) pp.60
Butter, carpets & upholstery pp.16, pp.39
Butter/Margarine, washable fabric pp.39

C

Candle Wax pp.61
Candle Wax, carpets & upholstery pp.16
Candle Wax, silver pp.16
Candle Wax, wood pp.16
Canvas Bags pp.61
Carpets & Upholstery pp.17
Carpets, stain removal musts pp.17
Casserole/Pie Dishes pp.47
Cast Iron Pans pp.47
Ceramic pp.17
Chalk pp.61
Chalk, wallpaper pp.17
Charcoal, colourfast fabrics pp.61
Chewing Gum pp.17, pp.61
Chewing Gum, carpets & upholstery pp.39
Chewing Gum, washable fabrics pp.39
Chlorine Bleach pp.5
Chocolate pp.61
Chocolate, carpets pp.18, pp.40
Chocolate, washable fabric pp.40
Cigarette Burns, wood pp.18
Coffee & Tea Pots pp.47
Coffee & Tea pp.40

Coffee & Tea, carpets & upholstery pp.18, pp.40
Coffee & Tea, countertops pp.41
Coffee Makers, glass or stainless steel pp.47
Coffee Tables, pp.18
Coffee, fresh stains pp.41, pp.62
Cooking Oil pp.47, pp.62
Cooking Oil, washable fabrics pp.41
Cooking Oil, worktops & hobs pp.41
Copper Stains pp.31
Cornflour pp.9
Crayon pp.62
Crayon, carpets pp.18
Crayon, painted walls pp.19
Crayon, wallpaper pp.19
Cream of Tartar pp.10
Cream, washable fabrics pp.41
Curry pp.62
Curry, carpets pp.19, pp.42
Curry, washable fabrics pp.42
Cutlery pp.48

D

Deodorant/Antiperspirant pp.63
Dirt, carpets pp.19
Dishwasher pp.48
Dog Collars pp.81
Dry Cleaning Fluid pp.6
Duvets pp.20
Dye Stains pp.88

E

Egg pp.63
Egg, washable fabrics pp.42
Eggs, hard floors pp.48
Enamel Pans pp.48
Extractor Fans pp.31, pp.48

F

Face Cloths pp.63
Faeces, carpets & upholstery pp.82
Faeces, washable fabric pp.82
Felt Tip Pen pp.20, pp.63
Floor Tiles pp.20, pp.31, pp.48
Food Colouring pp.63
Food Colouring, washable fabrics pp.42
Foundation, makeup pp.63
Fruit & Fruit Juice pp.20
Fruit & Fruit Juice, on carpets pp.43
Fruit Juice pp.43, pp.64
Fruit pp.64
Fruit, dried on stains pp.64
Fruit, dried on stains/washable fabrics pp.43
Fruit, washable fabrics pp.42

G

Garden Furniture, resin stains pp.77
Glass Decanters pp.20
Glass Stains pp.65
Glasses pp.49
Glue (PVA) pp.64
Glue, table & chair joints pp.78
Glycerine pp.6
Grass Stains pp.78
Grease, carpets pp.21
Grease, fresh stains pp.65
Grease, hands pp.78
Grease, pathways, driveways & garage floors pp.21
Grease, suede pp.66
Grease, wallpaper pp.21
Grease/Oil, concrete pp.78
Greasy Fingers, wooden furniture pp.21
Grill Pans pp.49
Grout pp.31
Grout pp.49

H

Hair Dye pp.66
Handkerchiefs pp.66
Hard Water Spots, stainless steel pp.21, pp.32, pp.49
Heat Marks, light coloured wooden furniture pp.21
Heat Marks, polished furniture pp.22
Home Entertainment Systems pp.22
Hydrogen Peroxide pp.6

I

Ice Cream, carpets pp.22, pp.43
Ice Cream, on washable fabrics pp.43
Ink pp.66
Ink, carpets & upholstery pp.22
Ink, walls pp.22
Iodine pp.66
Iron Plate, rusty pp.23
Iron Plate, stains pp.23
Ironing & Stains pp.66

J

Jam pp.67
Jam, washable fabrics pp.44

K

Kitchen Counters pp.49
Kitchen Tiles pp.49
Knives Rust pp.49

L

Leather pp.23
Lemon Juice pp.10
Limescale pp.32, pp.50
Lipstick pp.22, pp.67
Lipstick, glasses or china pp.23
Liquids, carpets pp.23

M

Make-up pp.67
Marble Counters pp.23, pp.50
Mascara pp.68
Mattresses pp.24
Mayonnaise pp.68
Mayonnaise, washable fabrics pp.44
Melted Plastic pp.50
Methylated Spirits pp.7
Microwaves pp.50
Mild Bleaching Agents pp.55
Mildew, on clothes pp.68
Mildew, shower curtains pp.32
Mildew/Damp Stains, walls/ceiling/tiles pp.32
Milk, washable fabrics pp.44
Milk/Cream/Butter pp.68
Mould pp.32, pp.68
Mud pp.68
Mud, carpets pp.24

Index

N

Nail Polish pp.69
Nappies pp.69
Newspaper print pp.69
Nicotene pp.24
Non-Stick Pans pp.51

O

Oil & Grease pp.69
Oil & Grease, heavy oils pp.69
Oil & Grease, light oils pp.69
Oil-Based Stains pp.88
Ovens & Hobs pp.51
Ovens pp.51

P

Paint (Oil-based) pp.70
Paint (Water-based) pp.70
Paint, glass pp.24, pp.79
Paint, wallpaper pp.24, pp.79
Pasta Sauce (Tomato), washable fabrics pp.111
Pasta Sauce pp.70
Pencil Marks, lead pp.70
Perfume pp.70
Permanent Ink/Marker, carpet pp.24
Permanent Ink/Marker, countertops pp.24
Perspiration pp.71
Pet Urine, on concrete pp.82
Pollen pp.71
Pollen, carpets pp.25
Porcelain/Enamel Bath & Sinks pp.33
Protein Stains pp.86

Q

Quilted or Down Jackets pp.71

R

Red Wine, carpets pp.25, pp.44
Red Wine, fresh stains pp.71
Red Wine, older stains pp.71
Red Wine, washable fabrics pp.44
Rubbing Alcohol pp.7
Running Colours, silk, wool & delicates pp.72
Running Colours, white cotton or linen pp.72
Rust Stains, around baths pp.33
Rust, baking trays pp.52
Rust, metal pp.25
Rust, white cotton pp.72
Rusty Tools pp.80

S

Saliva pp.10

Salt pp.11

Scorch Marks pp.72

Scuff Marks, vinyl pp.26

Sealant, mould & stains pp.33

Shirt Collars & Cuffs pp.72

Shoe Polish pp.72

Shoe Polish, carpets pp.26

Shoes, leather pp.26

Shoes, suede pp.26

Shower Stalls pp.34

Silver pp.26

Soap Scum pp.34

Soft Drinks pp.73

Soft Drinks, washable fabrics pp.44

Soot, brick pp.26

Soot, carpets pp.27

Stain Types pp.86

Standard Stain Remover pp.27

Sticky Labels, general pp.27

Sticky Labels, glass pp.27

Sticky Labels, plastic pp.27

Strong Bleaching Agents pp.55

Strong Scouring Powder pp.28, pp.34, pp.52

Suede pp.28

Sunlight pp.11

Super-Strong Scouring Powder pp.28, pp.34, pp.52

T

Tannin Stains pp.87

Taps pp.34, pp.52

Tar pp.73

Tar, shoes pp.28

Tea pp.73

Tea Towels pp.74

Tea, washable fabrics pp.45

Tea/Coffee Stains, countertops pp.52

Telephone Receivers pp.53

Thermos Flasks pp.53

Tidemarks pp.35

Ties pp.74

Timber floors (without hard finish) pp28

Tobacco pp.74

Toilets pp.35

Toilets, limescale pp.35

Tomato Sauce/Ketchup pp.45, pp.74

Tupperware pp.53

Turpentine pp.7

U

Urine (Pets), carpets & upholstery pp.29, pp.81
Urine pp.75, pp.82
Urine, mattresses pp.29

V

Vases pp.30
Vomit pp.75, pp.81

W

Wash Basins/Sinks pp.36
Washing Machines pp.54
Washing-Up Liquid pp.54
Water Marks pp.36, pp.76
Water Marks, carpets pp30
Water Marks, light coloured wooden furniture
pp.30
Water Marks, mahogany pp.30
White Cotton & Linen pp.76
White Porcelain Sinks pp.36, pp.54
White Spirit pp.8
White vinegar pp.11
White Wine pp.45, pp.76
Wooden Decking, mildew pp.80
Wooden Decking, oil stains pp.80

Index

Where you see this symbol, you will find 'eco friendly' solutions.

95

Spoons to millilitres

1/2 Teaspoon	2.5ml	1 Tablespoon	15ml
1 Teaspoon	5ml	2 Tablespoons	30ml
1-1/2 Teaspoons	7.5ml	3 Tablespoon	45ml
2 Teaspoons	10 ml	4 Tablespoons	60ml

Grams to Ounces

10g	0.25oz	225g	8oz
15g	0.38oz	250g	9oz
25g	1oz	275g	10oz
50g	2oz	300g	11oz
75g	3oz	350g	12oz
110g	4oz	375g	13oz
150g	5oz	400g	14oz
175g	6oz	425g	15oz
200g	7oz	450g	16oz

Metric to Cups

Flour etc	115g	1 cup
Clear Honey etc	350g	1 cup
Liquids	225ml	1 cup

Liquid measures

5fl oz	1/4 pint	150ml
7.5fl oz		215ml
10fl oz	1/2 pint	275ml
15fl oz		425ml
20fl oz	1 pint	570ml
35fl oz	1-3/4 pints	1 litre